THE WAY OF WISDOM

PROVERBS: A HANDBOOK FOR REARING WISE SONS (AND DAUGHTERS)

WAYNE T. CHRISTENSEN

Xulon PRESS

The Way Of Wisdom
Proverbs: A Handbook For Rearing Wise Sons
(And Daughters)
by Wayne T. Christensen

Printed in the United States of America

ISBN 9781609572945

www.xulonpress.com

To Chele

"An excellent wife, who can find?
For her worth is far above jewels."

Contents

Preface

The modern evangelical church is in the midst of a dire spiritual crisis. Statistics reveal that 70 to 88% of children who grew up in the church are abandoning church involvement by the end of their freshmen year of college. Reversing the tide of this mass exodus will not happen by merely tweaking our present system of discipleship or by piling on yet another program. All of us in the church must admit that we aren't just slightly wide of the bull's-eye—we are missing the target altogether.

Many reasons could be enumerated to explain why droves of children are turning their backs on the faith, but I believe that at the core, it is the result of the failure of *parents* to bring their children "up in the discipline and instruction of the Lord" (Eph. 6:4). After all, it is fathers and mothers who are charged to disciple their children. Following the giving of the Law, parents were instructed to pass on to their children the Law they had received: "'And these words that I command you today shall be on your heart. You shall teach them diligently to your children, and shall talk of them when you sit in your house, and when you walk by the way, and when you lie down, and when you rise'" (Deut. 6:6-7).

Perhaps, the most precious proverb of all for parents is Proverbs 22:6: "Train up a child in the way he should go; even when he is old he will not depart from it." However, before we hastily and presumptuously "claim the promise" we should ask a soul-searching question: Are we "training up" our children as God commands? Or, if the truth be told, have we abdicated our calling, and turned the discipleship of our children over to ministry leaders and the paid professionals? God's Word is unambiguous in stating that parents have the primary responsibility to tell "the coming generation the glorious deeds of the LORD, and his might, and the wonders that he has done" (Ps. 78:4).

The apostle Paul tells us that "All Scripture is breathed out by God and profitable for teaching, for reproof, for correction, and for training in righteousness, that the man of God may be competent, equipped for every good work" (2 Tim. 3:16-17). At the same time, the book of Proverbs is specifically designed for the discipleship of our sons and daughters. You may not find "education" listed in your concordance, but if you broaden your search to include "son" or "sons" references in Proverbs occur in great abundance. And for good reason, as its main purpose is for teaching children: "To know wisdom and instruction, to understand words of insight, to receive instruction in wise dealing" (Pro. 1:2-3). Therefore, I believe parents should be rigorously intentional about teaching Proverbs to their children.

Rearing wise children in an age of foolishness requires concerted effort and thoughtfulness. Practically, this means that parents must set aside time from the daily demands of life to disciple their children. I don't care if you call it "devotions," or "quiet time," or "family worship," I don't care if you do it in the morning or the evening, so long as you implement some time together reading and meditating on God's Word. As with a beautiful garden, weeds can spring up automatically without any effort on our part. But the precious fruit of wise, God-glorifying children demands strenuous cultivation. My hope and prayer is that this book will aid parents as they fulfill their mandate to disciple their children and bring them up in the ways of the Lord.

The subtitle of this book is *Proverbs: A Handbook for Rearing Wise Son (and Daughters).* I must confess, however, that it is a hodgepodge handbook. Some chapters were originally written as sermons, while others were written as weekly devotionals for our church body. Hopefully this final draft is cohesive enough to not annoy the reader as we move abruptly from one topic to the next. Even if it does have this feel from time to time, the reader shouldn't be too critical, since the book of Proverbs itself moves abruptly from one concern to the next without warning. What holds this book together, as well as the book of Proverbs, is its broad range of topics designed for rearing wise sons and daughters. May your children be numbered among the wise who bring joy to you as parents.

This book is the result of a collaborative effort, so please indulge me as I thank some of those who have come along side me to bring it to completion. I am very grateful to Bob Bakus' keen editorial eye and trusty red pen. Thanks also go to Sue Biegon who spent countless hours making corrections, as well as typing the tedious end notes and the Scripture index. I would be remiss not to express my gratitude to Mark and Elisa McClellan for their encouraging partnership in this publication, even though they will be embarrassed by their inclusion here. I thank the congregation of Fox Lake Community Church. So many of you were very eager to apply the glorious truths contained in the book of Proverbs in your own families. The dedication many of you show in discipling your children rebukes me and challenges me to do the same. And finally, I must join our children, Jacy, Jimmy, Lydia, Caleb and Zach, and rise up and call my wife, Michele, *blessed* for her hard work, energetic support, and persistent prayers. Chele, you truly embody the beauty, strength, and holiness of the Proverbs 31 woman.

Soli Deo Gloria.

WAYNE T. CHRISTENSEN

1

Truth, Goodness, & Beauty

A Look at How Proverbs Teaches Biblical Truth

When it comes to teaching children fundamental doctrine, the *Westminster Shorter Catechism*, for example, is excellent. The question and answer format is great for indoctrination, as the following story from the life of Dwight L. Moody illustrates. "Moody, the famous nineteenth century evangelist, was preaching once to a crowded meeting of children in Edinburgh, Scotland. To get their attention he posed a question: 'What is prayer?'—expecting to answer the question himself. But to his amazement scores of little hands went up all over the hall. So Moody asked one young fellow to give his answer. The boy spoke out with clear and confident tones, 'Prayer is an offering up of our desires unto God for things agreeable to His will, in the name of Christ, with confession of our sins and thankful acknowledgment of His mercies.' Moody's amazed response was, 'Thank God, my boy, that you were born in Scotland!'"[1] This is the kind of doctrinal clarity that catechizing can produce.

However, with fear and trepidation, if I can be just a little critical of the *WSC*, despite its obvious strength for providing solid answers to biblical questions (which I use with my own kids and church), it is terribly dry at points. I wasn't surprised when I learned that it was written by a mathematician. I have nothing against mathematicians, mind you, but the *WSC* can read like the Pythagorean theorem at times. The bare bones of doctrine also need flesh and blood if doctrine is going to be living and active, so as to transform lives. Remember, the desired end of all theology is transformation, not just information. Henry David Thoreau warned, "A fact stated barely is dry. It must be the vehicle of some humanity in order to interest us. It is like giving a man a stone when he asks you for bread." In a similar vein, poet Richard Hugo wrote, "I caution against communication because once language exists only to convey information, it is dying."

Before delving into the book of Proverbs proper, I'd like us to consider *how* its authors (usually Solomon) passed on wisdom and insight to their sons. And it's important to clarify that wisdom in Proverbs cannot be reduced to learning a set of propositions. Wisdom is not merely about regurgitating the correct answers on the final exam; rather wisdom manifests itself in a life of righteousness, justice, and equity (Pro. 1:3). *What* we teach is critical—our doctrine must be orthodox; however, here we want to focus on *how* biblical truth is communicated to sons (and of course this would apply to daughters as well, but Proverbs specifically addresses sons).

I went to a pastor's conference once where the speaker said from the outset that he wasn't going to use any illustrations or applications, he was just going to "give us the Word." I interpreted his words as, "This is going to be a dull, lifeless lecture. Grab a pillow." Actually, it wasn't too bad, but it would have been far better if he had included illustrations and applications. I'm not advocating for what Charles H. Spurgeon called skyscraper sermons, where the speaker gives you nothing but one story on top of another. That's the opposite extreme—spineless sermons. The balance is rock-solid biblical teaching presented in a vivid fashion, so that it informs the mind, provokes the imagination, stirs the emotions, and moves the will toward greater holiness.

It's relatively easy to teach our children to discern between truth and error, as well as between good and bad. Even new converts know that pride, anger, lust, greed, and envy are bad. Yet, how many Christians at any age view pride, anger, lust, greed, and envy as ugly and disgusting, so that they have a visceral reaction that causes them to instinctively veer away from these repulsive sins? How many Christians "worship the LORD in the *beauty* of holiness"? (Ps. 29:2, KJV, emphasis added). Truth, goodness, *and beauty* are essential to godly living.

We Christians have done a fairly good job of emphasizing *truth* and *goodness*, but we have failed to captivate the next generation with the *beauty* of the Christian life, which helps to bridge the gap between information and application. "Walter Brueggemann speaks for all of us when he says, 'I have found myself discovering that mostly I do not need more advice, but strength. I do not need new information, but the courage, freedom and authorization to act on what I already have been given in the gospel… The deep places in our lives—places of resistance and embrace—are not ultimately reached by instruction. Those places of resistance and embrace are reached only by stories, by images, metaphors and phrases that line out the world differently, apart from our fear and hurt.'"[2]

Is Brueggemann correct in saying that stories, images, metaphors, and phrases can reach the deep places of resistance and embrace in our lives in a way that information by itself can't? I believe he is, and that is precisely the thesis of this introduction, and it is one of the great indirect lessons about teaching that we learn from the book of Proverbs.

Proverbs provides us with a window to peer through, as we observe how godly parents instruct their children in the Scriptures, so that they, LORD-willing, will walk in paths of righteousness and integrity. And what we see taking place in Proverbs is not catechizing, but a more graphic and lively kind of instruction. Consider a couple of examples by way of comparison.

Exodus 20:12, the fifth commandment, says, '"Honor your father and your mother, that your days may be long in the land that the LORD your God is giving you."' God's Word often teaches nonnegotiable, propositional truths, so it obviously isn't wrong for us to teach this way either. Nevertheless, the vast majority of the Bible doesn't present us with naked "Thou shalt not" declarations, but narratives. Now notice how Proverbs teaches the fifth commandment: "The eye that mocks a father and scorns to obey a mother will be picked out by the ravens of the valley and eaten by the vultures" (Pro. 30:17). Would you not agree that this image reaches the deep places of resistance in a way that the fifth commandment alone doesn't?

Consider another comparison. The seventh commandment says, '"You shall not commit adultery"' (Ex. 20:14). Will just teaching our children to memorize this commandment guarantee marital bliss and fidelity? If it were only that simple, right? In addition to this commandment, we should also (again, notice that it's not either/or but both/and) tell our sons, "Lust not after her beauty in thine heart; neither let her take thee with her eyelids. For by means of a whorish woman a man is brought to a piece of bread: and the adulteress will hunt for the precious life. Can a man take fire in his bosom, and his clothes not be burned? Can one go upon hot coals, and his feet not be burned?" (Pro. 6:25-28, KJV). A friend of mine was in a store by himself on one occasion, and he was tempted to browse through some pornographic magazines that caught his attention—that is, until God brought this

Proverb to mind, and he thought to himself, "If I give in to this temptation I'll be toast!" By the grace of God he walked away unscathed. Proverbs provides this kind of right-brain imaginative instruction that our children need for holiness.

Never underestimate the power of your child's imagination. David Mills is correct: "We tend to rely, I think, too much on knowledge. Even if Johnny has memorized the *Baltimore Catechism* or the *Westminster Confession*, or even hundreds of verses of Scripture, if his imagination has been formed by the wider, secular culture, he will respond to temptations as a secularist, not as a Christian.

"He will *know* that fornication is wrong and that intercourse is a gift reserved for marriage, but will *feel* that it is a recreational activity to be enjoyed with a willing partner by someone of sufficient maturity to use 'protection'—though the Christian teaching may affect him enough that he feels it requires some degree of 'commitment.' When he brings himself to temptation, his feelings are more likely to move him than his thoughts, and of course once he falls, his thoughts will start to change to fit his feelings."[3] This is why our children's imaginations must be shaped by good stories—the only alternative of course is bad stories. But stories are not just a matter of good entertainment verses bad entertainment. Children will interpret the world around them through the grid that stories provide, and in addition to this they will behave like the characters in the stories that they identify with the most.

Mills goes on to say, "What we want our children to imagine depends upon what we want our children to be. As Christians, we want them not just to learn to understand and analyze rightly, but to react rightly because they see the world rightly. We want our children to know by instinct or intuition what is the right answer, the right action, the right attitude.

"Revulsion is a much better protection from the force of the passions than an intellectual understanding by itself. To feel 'This is yucky' is not a final protection from sin, but it is better than thinking 'This is wrong' but feeling 'This is okay.' Lust offers the paradigmatic case (examples come quickly to mind), but this is true of pride, gluttony, envy, and all the rest, even sloth."[4]

Without the right stories our knowledge will conflict with our feelings. And, as Mills implied, our knowledge usually gives way to our feelings, our desires. Jonathan Edwards concurs: "A man never, in any instance, wills any thing contrary to his desires… *It is that motive, [i.e., desire] which, as it stands in the view of the mind, is the strongest, that determines the will.*"[5] In other words, our decisions are determined by the strongest desires of the moment.

We like to think that we make decisions based upon our intellect. We like to think most of our choices are the result of reasonable, rational reflections. The pros and cons are carefully weighed on the scale, and then we make our decision. But do we? If this is so, why do we "decide" to watch TV instead of reading the Bible, when the scale clearly tilts in the direction of the latter? Why do we "decide" to sleep in on Sunday morning, rather than go to church? Because of a biblically-informed, conscious decision? Doubtful! Most daily decisions, including decisions to sin, result from something much deeper within us. We are driven by desires, which are fueled by stories, as well as images, music, video games, people we come into contact with, etc.—which are really all part of the larger story.

This is elementary, but powerful, so I'd like to flesh it out with a couple of examples. Many years ago now, a college freshman approached me after a sermon about a verse I had referred to in passing. The verse was Ephesians 5:4: "Let there be no filthiness nor foolish talk nor crude joking, which are out of place, but instead let there be thanksgiving." This student, who grew up in the church by the way, confessed that Ephesians 5:4 was an apt description of the conversations that he and his friends had on a regular basis. For a generation that has grown up watching perverse sitcoms, placing themselves habitually in those kinds of stories (we can't help but do this), the natural outcome will be relating to one another in a way that mirrors the stories: sexual innuendos, crude humor, putting others down, no respect for authority, and nonstop joking. Observe how kids, or adults for that matter, relate to each other. Rarely do they have serious or civil conversations; most of the time they entertain each other as though they're performing in a "*Simpsons*" episode. Hollywood likes to say that it merely reflects culture, but the truth is that Hollywood is also creating a particular culture by the stories it tells. And the stories (which take place in imaginary places) that we live in for extended periods of time end up transferring to the real world in which we live.

A frightening example of how this works comes from the 1999 Columbine High School massacre by two students, Eric Harris and Dylan Klebold. The shooting ended with the deaths of 12 students and a teacher, as well as the wounding of 24 others before Eric and Dylan committed suicide. Sociologists, psychologists, and psychiatrists too debate the exact cause of the rampage, but it's clear that the stories of their world were very dark, from its gothic culture to its heavy metal music to its violent video games. After the tragedy, I heard an interview with a federal official expressing his sheer amazement at how calm Eric and Dylan had been. He mentioned that trained FBI field agents would have had difficulty being as calm as the two students were, due to the adrenal rush that such an intense situation would normally produce. In his opinion, the two students had steady trigger fingers, because years of playing violent video games was like simulator training for such a killing. He went on to say that their calm, one-shot-per-person approach exactly mimicked a video game. My conclusion is that their incredible calmness was due to, what I will call, "story transfer." They merely transferred the video story on the screen to the real story at the school. And it's horrifying how easily that transfer occurred.

Proverbs declares, "For as he thinketh in his heart, so is he" (Pro. 23:7a, KJV). I hope by now we see that this thinking is far deeper than the recitation of Bible verses, however good that may be; it also involves the imagination. As parents, our goal is *not* to get our children to conform to a biblical standard of righteousness—that's relatively easy to do with a big stick. Our goal is to get our children to *love* the standard. If they don't love the standard, they will quickly abandon it once they are out on their own, which statistics tell us most church kids are doing in droves. This means that graphic and lively stories, images, metaphors, and phrases, which Proverbs liberally employs, are not optional, but essential for demonstrating the truth, goodness, and beauty of the Christian life, so that any other way of living will seem sickening and repulsive by comparison.

2

Get Wisdom; Get Insight

The Purpose of the Book of Proverbs

When my son, Caleb, was 4 years old, I asked him what he wanted to be when he grew up. He said he wanted to be an ice cream man, a pastor, and a candy man. What did you want to be? How come nobody ever—or rarely—says that when he or she grows up he or she wants to be a sage; a wise person? We want to be rich, famous, good- looking, well-educated, successful, etc. But how many pursue knowledge and wisdom as the great objective of their life?

The purpose for which Proverbs was written is clear from the introduction: "To know wisdom and instruction, to understand words of insight, to receive instruction in wise dealing" (Pro. 1:2-3). Basically, Proverbs is a compilation of practical wisdom from a father to his son(s), to enable him (them) to live in a way that pleases and glorifies God. This is why we find the repeated refrain "my son(s)" throughout the book (1:8; 2:1; 3:1; 4:1; 5:1; 6:1; 7:1). This father (usually Solomon) is endeavoring to pass on to his son(s) what his father (David) gave to him. Solomon writes, "Hear, O sons, a father's instruction, and be attentive, that you may gain insight... When I was a son with my father, tender, the only one in the sight of my mother, he taught me and said to me, 'Let your heart hold fast my words; keep my commandments, and live. Get wisdom; get insight; do not forget, and do not turn away from the words of my mouth'" (4:1, 3-5). The burden of this father is to raise wise and insightful children.

Parents, what aspirations or dreams do you have for your children? One study revealed that even Christian parents were more concerned about the education their children received than they were about their spiritual growth. It's unfortunate that we have such a dichotomy in our thinking, because education, whether we realize it or not, is fundamentally religious. So when we talk about education and spiritual growth, this is a distinction without a difference. We need to think long and hard about why we're sending our children to school in the first place, even if that means sending them to the kitchen table for home schooling.

During the Mexican-American War (c. 1847), Robert E. Lee wrote this letter to his eldest son Custis: "'I thought of you, my dear Custis, on the 18th in the battle [of Cerro Gordo], and wondered, when the musket balls and grape were whistling over my head in a perfect shower, where I could put you, if with me, to be safe. I was truly thankful that you were at school, I hope learning to be good and wise. You have no idea what a horrible sight a battlefield is.'"[6] I know this is just a passing point in Gen. Lee's letter, so I may be reading into his comments, but he hoped that Custis' school would help him to be good and wise, and not just learn reading, writing, and arithmetic, so he could qualify for a great, high-paying job some day.

Imagine your son or daughter going off to college. At the beginning of your teenage child's first day of class, the professor says, "I want to be very clear about the purpose for which you are being educated at this university, so let me read to you from our handbook." Then he reads, "Let every student be plainly instructed, and earnestly pressed to consider well, the main end of his life and studies is, to know God and Jesus Christ which is eternal life, John 17:3, and therefore to lay Christ in the bottom, as the only foundation of all sound knowledge and learning. And seeing the LORD only gives wisdom, let every one seriously set himself by prayer in secret to seek it of him, Proverbs 2:3." With this understanding of education, what kind of college would you think your child had enrolled in? Some conservative Bible college? The professor has just read to the students from the rules and precepts that were to govern Harvard, adopted Sept. 26, 1642.

If you want to be proud of your children when they are grown, see that they are educated to be good and wise when they're young. "A wise son makes a glad father, but a foolish son is a sorrow to his mother" (Pro. 10:1). If any motif binds all the proverbs together, it is the antithesis between the wise man and the fool. And it is plain that you will be either one or the other. "The wise of heart will receive commandments, but a babbling fool will come to ruin" (10:8). "The way of a fool is right in his own eyes, but a wise man listens to advice" (12:15).

Bear in mind that a fool is not necessarily stupid or uneducated or unintelligent; a fool can be very erudite and learned. Rather a fool is one who has no reverence for God; he is irreligious. "The fool says in his heart, 'There is no God.' They are corrupt, they do abominable deeds, there is none who does good" (Ps. 14:1). Inevitably, when you don't fear God, it will show in how you live; as will fear of the LORD, which is the beginning of wisdom (Pro. 9:10).

The Blessings Wisdom Holds Out to Us

To motivate us in our pursuit of lady wisdom, Proverbs tells us that nothing we desire compares to her, and that she holds out numerous blessings for those who seek her out. "Blessed is the one who finds wisdom, and the one who gets understanding, for the gain from her is better than gain from silver and her profit better than gold. She is more precious than jewels, and nothing you desire can compare with her. Long life is in her right hand; in her left hand are riches and honor" (3:13-16).

The wise are blessed, because they find wisdom. And they found it not because they accidentally tripped over it, while they were chasing after something else such as wealth, but because they were diligently and prayerfully striving to attain it. Do you prize wisdom? Do you see its value? It's easy to say yes, since that's obviously the right answer, but is there any discipline in your life that testifies to this fact? One Christian man I know of listens to the Bible on CD on the way to work, another listens to sermons. How is your commitment to the depository of wisdom, the Word of God?

Jonathan Edwards included this resolution among his 70 well-known resolutions: "Resolved, to study the Scriptures so steadily, constantly and frequently, as that I may find, and plainly perceive myself to grow in the knowledge of the same." Can we see clearly that our systematic study of God's Word is resulting in greater knowledge? This is not to be a guessing game: "I think I see growth." Our growth should be obvious, because we "plainly perceive" that our reading and studying have led to greater insight into God's will and being.

Kids, how well do you listen when your parents instruct you, whether it's about friends or homework or politics? If you really treasure wisdom and understanding, you will listen carefully and not presume to have all the answers. Imagine your mom and dad saying, "Come into the kitchen, we have a gift for you," and as you look at the table heaping with silver, gold, and precious stones, they say, "We've been saving our whole lives to pass this on to you." How would you respond? *That* should be your attitude when your parents instruct you, because according to God, wisdom and understanding are even more profitable and precious than mounds of money.

I know what some of you are thinking: "But I really want to be wealthy." I didn't say that you had to choose between wisdom and wealth, I just said that wisdom is more valuable than wealth. Wisdom *always* leads to blessings, which *may* include riches. Wisdom often leads to wealth, but pursuing wealth doesn't usually lead to wisdom—so be careful.

One night King Solomon received the invitation of a lifetime. "In that night God appeared to Solomon, and said to him, 'Ask what I shall give you'" (2 Chr. 1:7). What would you have asked for? The winning numbers to the lottery? Long life? Fame? "Solomon requested, 'Give me now wisdom and knowledge to go out and come in before this people, for who can govern this people of yours, which is so great?' God answered Solomon, 'Because this was in your heart, and you have not asked possessions, wealth, honor, or the life of those who hate you, and have not even asked long life, but have asked wisdom and knowledge for yourself that you may govern my people over whom I have made you king, wisdom and knowledge are granted to you. I will also give you riches, possessions, and honor, such as none of the kings had who were before you, and none after you shall have the like'" (vv. 10-12). Again, we see that wisdom leads to wealth and all the other blessings of God, and not the reverse.

Parents, do you want your children to be blessed; to enjoy long life, riches, and honor? Then do whatever it takes ("Though it cost all you have" [Pro. 4:7; NIV]) to turn your sons (and daughters) into philosophers. And do your best to become a philosopher yourself. What's a philosopher? Let me give you a simple definition, before mental images of Aristotle and Plato come flooding to the forefront of your mind, along with difficult-to-remember Latin phrases, such as "*Cogito, ergo sum.*" (In case you're wondering, it means, "I think, therefore I am." The concept was introduced by the seventeenth century philosopher René Descartes.) The word "philosophy" is made up of two Greek words, "philos," which means love, and "sophia," which means wisdom. Thus a philosopher is simply a person who loves wisdom. R.C. Sproul noted that the Queen of Sheba, having heard of Solomon's wisdom, traveled over 1,400 miles to test him and evaluate his wisdom for herself, but we will not even cross the street. A philosopher makes the trek.

3

A Wise Son Fears God

A Look at the Foundation of Wisdom and Ethics

"A wise son makes a glad father, but a foolish son is a sorrow to his mother" (Pro. 10:1). Imagine that your son (or daughter) fulfills his dream of becoming a doctor or a lawyer or a major league baseball player, but he lives like a fool. He rejects God's counsel. He associates with men whose paths are crooked. He is seduced by the adulteress woman with her flattering words. His lust for money leads to a gambling problem and high-risk investments, which ends in bankruptcy. The net result is shame. Remember, a *wise* son makes a glad father—not a wealthy son or a successful son or a famous son.

Since rearing wise children is so crucial, where do we begin? We don't have to guess. "The fear of the LORD is the *beginning* of knowledge; fools despise wisdom and instruction… The fear of the LORD is the *beginning* of wisdom, and the knowledge of the Holy One is insight" (Pro. 1:7; 9:10, emphasis added). We will not even begin to impart wisdom to our children without a healthy fear of God. Many assume that the fear of the LORD is for the mature, but Solomon tells us that it is for everybody who wants to acquire wisdom, including children. And, in a profound sense, anyone who fears the LORD already has wisdom. "'Behold, the fear of the Lord, that is wisdom,'" (Job 28:28).

Some reject the fear of the LORD by citing 1 John 4:18, as if this verse trumps all the verses on the fear of God and cancels them out. We need to keep in mind that 1 John 4:18 is dealing with a specific issue, namely "the day of judgment" (1 Jn. 4:17). "There is no fear in love, but perfect love casts out fear. For fear has to do with punishment, and whoever fears has not been perfected in love" (vs. 18). To be sure God doesn't want his children to be terrorized by the prospect of judgment and damnation. The whole book of first John was written, according to 5:13, "to you who believe in the name of the Son of God that you may know that you have eternal life." At the same time this doesn't absolve us of a sense of reverence and awe we should have in the presence of a majestic and holy God. The writer of Hebrews exhorts us, "let us offer to God acceptable worship, with reverence and awe, for our God is a consuming fire" (Heb. 12:28-29).

The fear of the LORD is the foundation of wisdom, and it is also the foundation of ethics. "By the fear of the LORD one turns away from evil" (Pro. 16:6). Solomon concludes Ecclesiastes, "The end of the matter; all has been heard. Fear God and keep his commandments, for this is the whole duty of man" (Ecc. 12:13). Fearing God and keeping his commandments are not two unrelated commands, as we have already seen from Proverbs 16:6; it is precisely by fearing God that we are empowered to turn away from evil and walk in obedience.

Despite what our culture wants to believe, religion and ethics are inextricably linked. John Murray saw this connection. He said, "This emphasis which Scripture places upon the fear of God evinces the bond that exists between religion and ethics. The fear of God is essentially a religious concept; it refers to the conception we entertain of God and the attitude of heart and mind that is ours by reason of that conception. Since the biblical ethic is grounded in and is the fruit of the fear of the Lord, we are apprised again that ethics has its source in religion and as our religion is so will be our ethic. This is to say also that what or whom we worship determines our behavior."[7] Therefore, when there is a decline of religion in a country, with the fear of God at the heart of that religion, we should not be surprised if there is also a corresponding decline in morality and ethics. In fact, it is inescapable.

The fear of the Lord is to affect all we do. Even the most mundane activities find their impetus in the fear of the Lord. Consider a few examples. The fear of the Lord should motivate Christians to be conscientious and hard workers. "Slaves, obey in everything those who are your earthly masters, not by way of eye-service, as people-pleasers, but with sincerity of heart, fearing the Lord" (Col. 3:22). "Fearing the Lord" isn't a superfluous phrase; it is meant to be the main motivating factor in our work. Also, Spirit-filled Christians should be "submitting to one another out of reverence [literally, fear] for Christ" (Eph. 5:21). Finally, "And if you call on him as Father who judges impartially according to each one's deeds, conduct yourselves with fear throughout the time of your exile" (1 Pet. 1:17).

To raise God-fearing children is to raise children who reflect Christ. Isaiah prophesied of the Messiah, "And the Spirit of the LORD shall rest upon him…the Spirit of knowledge and the fear of the LORD. And his delight shall be in the fear of the LORD" (Isa. 11:2-3).

Raising God-fearing Children Once Again

There was a time when Christians in America were known as God-fearing people. Parents made it a priority to instill within their children a healthy fear of God. Today, such parenting is seen as archaic and outdated, if not cruel and barbaric. Why would any loving parent teach his or her children to fear God?

First, recognize, as we've said, that the fear of the LORD is the foundation of morality and ethics. Scripture often makes a connection between fearing God and avoiding evil. For example, the LORD commended Job before Satan for being '"a blameless and upright man, who fears God and turns away from evil"' (Job 1:8). Proverbs 8:13 says, "The fear the LORD is hatred of evil." Do you want your children to hate lying, cheating, stealing, immorality, disobedience, etc.? Then teach them to fear the LORD.

John Murray said, "The highest reaches of sanctification are realized only in the fear of God."[8] This is supported by 2 Corinthians 7:1, which exhorts us to "cleanse ourselves from all defilement of flesh and spirit, perfecting holiness *in the fear of God*" (NASB, emphasis added).

Paul strings together one Old Testament passage after another, in Romans 3:10-18, to drive home the point that we are all sinners in desperate need of a Savior. The climax and explanation for our sinfulness comes in verse 18: "There is no fear of God before their eyes." At the root of sin is a failure to fear God. The wicked could simply be defined as those who don't fear God. John Calvin astutely observed, "All wickedness flows from a disregard of God...Since the fear of God is the bridle by which our wickedness is held in check, its removal frees us to indulge in every kind of licentious conduct."

Second, realize that the fear of God is not to be equated with terror that would traumatize our children. There is a subtle, but crucial, distinction between being "afraid" of God and "fearing" God. I know this sounds like a semantics word game, so let me explain. In Exodus 20, God delivers the Ten Commandments from Mount Sinai amidst thunder, lightning, loud trumpet blasts, smoke and fire, as the mountain trembled violently due to His presence. "When the people saw the thunder and lightning and heard the trumpet and saw the mountain in smoke, they trembled with fear..." (vs. 18, NIV). "Moses said to the people, 'Do not be afraid. God has come to test you, so that the fear of God will be with you to keep you from sinning'" (vs. 20, NIV). The people are not to be *afraid* of God, but they are to *fear* God. Moses is not contradicting himself, but making a vital distinction. Verse 20 could be paraphrased: "Do not be *terrorized*. God has come to test you, so that *reverential awe* of God will be with you to keep you from sin."

John Calvin recognized this distinction: "Because it [i.e., the *pious mind* who sees the one and only true God] sees him to be a righteous judge, armed with severity to punish wickedness, it ever holds his judgment seat before its gaze, and through fear of him restrains itself from provoking his anger. And yet it is not so terrified by the awareness of his judgment as to wish to withdraw, even if some way of escape were open... Besides, this mind restrains itself from sinning, not out of dread of punishment alone; but, because it loves and reveres God as Father...and adores him as Lord...

"Here indeed is pure and real religion: faith so joined with an earnest fear of God that this fear also embraces willing reverence..."[9]

Third, note that the fear of God complements our love for God. God is not only to be our greatest love, but also our greatest fear (Lk. 12:4-5). Both should be embraced equally and simultaneously: "'And now, O Israel, what does the LORD your God ask of you but to *fear the LORD your God*, to walk in all his ways, to *love him...*,'" (Deut. 10:12, NIV, emphasis added). Fearing God without loving God will end in terror; a dreadful deity to hide from. Loving God without fearing God will end in sentimentalism; a domesticated deity to treat as an equal. Embracing both will cause us to come boldly into His presence with reverential awe.

In C.S. Lewis' book *The Lion, the Witch, and the Wardrobe*, Susan asks Mrs. Beaver about Aslan the Great Lion, who represents Christ.

> "Is he—quite safe? I shall feel rather nervous about meeting a lion."
> "That you will, dearie, and no mistake," said Mrs. Beaver; "if there's anyone who can appear before Aslan without their knees knocking, they're either braver than most or else just silly."
> "Then he isn't safe?" said Lucy.
> "Safe?" said Mr. Beaver; "don't you hear what Mrs. Beaver tells you? Who said anything about safe? 'Course he isn't safe. But he's good. He's the King, I tell you."

Considering the Relationship Between Love for God and Fear of God

If somebody were to ask me, "Should I be motivated to serve God because I love Him or because I fear Him?" My answer would be, "Yes." Both are biblical and necessary means of motivating God's people to live for Him, although love is clearly the greatest virtue and best means of motivation. For starters, we must realize that we are commanded both to love God (Deut. 6:5) and to fear God (1 Pet. 2:17) simultaneously. Obviously the inspired writers of Scripture didn't think these commands were contradictory or in conflict with each other, but could coexist harmoniously (Deut. 10:12).

Many passages of Scripture use love as a motivation to live for God. It motivates us to obey Him: '"If you love me, you will obey what I command"' (Jn. 14:15, 23, NIV).

Love for Christ encourages us to feed His flock: "'Yes, Lord' [Peter] said; 'you know that I love you.' Jesus said, 'Feed my lambs'" (Jn. 21:15, NIV).

On the other hand, many passages of Scripture show that fear of God is also a strong motivating factor in our walk with Christ. It motivates us to avoid sin: ""the fear of God will be with you to keep you from sinning"' (Ex. 20:20, NIV).

Fear motivates us to be submissive: "(S)ubmitting to one another out of reverence [literally "fear" as in the NASB] for Christ" (Eph. 5:21, NIV).

It inspires bold evangelism: "Since, then, we know what it is to fear the Lord, we try to persuade men" (2 Cor. 5:11; Matt. 10:27-28, NIV).

It gives us courage to defy ungodly governmental decrees: "The midwives, however, feared God and did not do what the king of Egypt had told them to do; they let the boys live" (even though they were commanded to kill them; Ex. 1:17, NIV). "And because the midwives feared God, he gave them families of their own" (vs. 21, NIV).

It is not impossible, as in Paul's case, in 2 Corinthians 5:11-15, to have love (vs. 14) and fear (vs.11) operating in conjunction with each other as twin motivating influences. The Bible often uses positive and negative motivations at the same time. One classic example is John 3:16: "For God so loved the world that he gave his one and only Son, that whoever believes in him shall not perish but have eternal life" (NIV). First, it contains the strongest negative motivation there is (hell —"shall not perish") to encourage us to put our faith in Christ. Jonathan Edwards said, "Some say it is unreasonable to frighten people into heaven. But I say it is reasonable to try to frighten people away from hell." Doesn't Jesus use vivid descriptions, such as, "And throw that worthless servant outside, into the darkness, where there will be weeping and gnashing of teeth" (Matt. 25:30, NIV), in part, to direct people away from hell? "Scare theology" did not originate with Jonathan Edwards.

John 3:16 also contains the strongest positive motivation there is (heaven—"but have eternal life") to exhort us to believe in Jesus. The Bible is literally loaded with both forceful threats of punishment and inspiring promises of reward to motivate faith and obedience.

Fear and love are the two basic motivations for children to obey their parents. Love is the greatest motive, and children are at their best when love compels them to obey and honor their father and mother. But if this love should diminish (and it certainly will from time to time), fear of chastisement may rise to the surface and enable the child to persevere with an obedient and honoring spirit. If they are not driven primarily by love, fear will suffice, though love is the highest virtue. It is no different for the children of God as they relate to their heavenly Father.

Jonathan Edwards described the relationship between love and fear this way (it will help to read this slowly): "For so hath God contrived and constituted things, in His dispensations towards His own people, that when their love decays, and the exercises of it fail or become weak, fear should arise; for then they need it to restrain them from sin, and to excite them to care for the good of their souls, and so to stir them up to watchfulness and diligence in religion. But God hath so ordered, that when love rises and is in vigorous exercise, then fear should vanish and be driven away; for then they need it not, having a higher and more excellent principle in exercise, to restrain them from sin and stir them up to their duty. There are no other principles which human nature is under the influence of, that will ever make men conscientious, but one of these two, *fear* or *love*... therefore God has wisely ordained, that these two opposite principles of love and fear should rise and fall, like the two opposite scales of a balance; when one rises the other sinks."[10]

4

Listen to Your Parents

Proverbs' First Exhortation for Sons

Proverbs begins with the purpose for which it was written: "To know wisdom and instruction…to give prudence to the simple, knowledge and discretion to the youth" (Pro. 1:2, 4). The fruit of such a wise life may include long life, riches, and honor (3:16). And this road that leads to wisdom *begins* with the fear of the Lord (1:7; 9:10).

In Proverbs 1:8 we have the first exhortation given to the son: "Hear, my son, your father's instruction, and forsake not your mother's teaching." Let's be clear—to "hear" a father's instruction is to *obey* it. We know this from the parallel thought in the second half of the verse: "forsake not your mother's teaching." Often a proverb will have two lines or halves that are synonymous in thought, with the second reinforcing the first.

Perhaps you've seen a scenario similar to this one—with somebody else's child, of course. Dad's instructions are ignored, and with much frustration he says, "Son, didn't you hear what I told you to do?" The barely audible, polite response is, "Yes, I heard you," which interpreted means, "Yes, I heard what you told me to do, but I didn't feel like doing it." I call this *polite* disobedience. *Rude* disobedience is when the son (or daughter) defiantly says, "I heard you, but I'm not about to do what you're telling me to do." But notice that whether the disobedience is polite or rude, it's still *disobedience*.

If I can summarize the first eight verses in Proverbs, they go something like this: I, Solomon, son of David, king of Israel, have written these words so that young people may acquire knowledge and wisdom. But for this to happen they must have a healthy fear of the LORD *and they must listen to their parents*.

At this point we're still laying the necessary foundation upon which a wise and prudent life can be built.

Proverbs was written to pass on wisdom to the next generation, but wisdom doesn't come through osmosis by watching TV or playing video games. It comes predominately through Mom and Dad. "My son, do not forget my teaching, but let your heart keep my commandments… Blessed is the one who finds wisdom, and the one who gets understanding" (3:1, 13). This is a theme we see interwoven throughout several chapters in Proverbs: Listen to your parents and gain wisdom… listen to your parents and gain wisdom…listen to your parents and gain wisdom (see also 1:8-20; 2:1-6; 4:1-5). And of course the converse is also true: Disregard your parents and remain a fool.

If children listen to their parents, what can they expect to receive? The answer is, in addition to knowledge and wisdom, *honor*. "Hear, my son, your father's instruction, and forsake not your mother's teaching, for they are a graceful garland for your head and pendants for your necks" (1:8-9). "Graceful garland" and "pendants" are ancient images of honor. Proverbs 4:8-9 can act as a commentary: "Prize her highly, and she will exalt you; she will honor you if you embrace her. She will place on your head a graceful garland; she will bestow on you a beautiful crown." As I think about the men and women that God has honored throughout Church history, and even today, the vast majority had tremendous respect for their parents, especially their father.

Now, I'd like to clarify a couple of verses that can be misunderstood and abused, namely Proverbs 3:5-6: "Trust in the LORD with all your heart, and do not lean on your own understanding. In all your ways acknowledge him, and he will make straight your paths." Some interpret this as, "Trust in the LORD *and not in your parents,*" but this ignores the broader context, where children are expressly commanded to follow their parents (3:1). Rather, we should understand that one of the ways we trust in the LORD is *by* listening to our parents.

Proverbs 3:7 provides a warning that some teenagers especially need to heed: "Be not wise in your own eyes." You might be familiar with the bell-shaped curve, where at one end younger children around 3 or 4 years old think their parents know almost everything. Then at the peak of the bell-shaped curve those around 17 or 18 sometimes think that they know it all (certainly far more than their unenlightened parents). Finally, at the other end of the curve, those around 21 or 22 conclude that their parents were really pretty smart after all. Mark Twain once remarked, "When I was 17, I thought my father was the dumbest man in the world. When I was 21, I was amazed at how much the old man had learned in 4 years!" Even half-way educated people have learned that the more you learn, the more you learn how much there is to learn. This results in humility and an openness to the counsel of others, such as one's parents who have learned a few things through the years. On the other hand, arrogance can blind a person to his or her own ignorance. Consequently, some people are so dumb that they're not even smart enough to know they're dumb.

Are You Old Enough to Make Your Own Decisions? [11]

Perhaps you're a teenager and you're thinking it's about time you moved beyond your parents' instruction. You're thinking, "I'm old enough to make my own decisions." There's a lot implied in that statement that you need to ponder.

First, it implies that at a certain age (say, 18), the counsel of your parents is no longer needed. Or, maybe what you're really saying is that your parents' counsel is no longer desired, because what you want is contrary to what they think is in your best interest.

Second, there's the implication that "my own decisions" are made in isolation from everybody else around me, and they affect only me. We are not islands unto ourselves. In reality—if we can get in touch with reality for a moment—there is no such thing as "my own decisions" for anybody at any age, since all our decisions affect those around us, which include our family, church, and community.

Third, it implies that I have now arrived and have enough wisdom, insight, and understanding to determine what is best for me. This kind of arrogant thinking discards scores of verses in Proverbs that teach, regardless of age, that "in an abundance of counselors there is safety" (11:14), and that "a wise man listens to advice" (12:15; see also 13:10; 15:22; 20:18). The irony is that "I'm old enough to make my own decisions" is a comment that an older, wiser person wouldn't be foolish enough to make.

Unfortunately, our culture and government have encouraged individualism and the right to make one's "own decisions" at certain ages. For example, at 17 you have the lawful right to watch R-rated movies regardless of what your parents think. At 18 or 21, depending on the state, you have the right to lust, gamble, or even fornicate with prostitutes. Our government has determined that any child at any age at any time during pregnancy (at least this is true of my home state of Illinois) has the right to get an abortion without parental consent. But in defense of the government, I must hasten to add that the government doesn't allow minors to take aspirin without parental consent. Our courts even grant 12-year-olds, with all their vast wisdom, the right to divorce their parents.

"Well, at what age is a person old enough to make their own decisions?" you ask. Consider the age of the son in Proverbs. We're not told his exact age, but we are given some clues. For instance, we know that he is old enough to have wealth, produce, barns, and vats. His father admonishes him, "Honor the Lord with your wealth and with the firstfruits of all your produce; then your barns will be filled with plenty, and your vats will be bursting with wine" (3:9-10). This eliminates most 15-year-olds, even most 25-year-olds. Also, he is old enough to be married (5:18). Amazingly, his father gives him marital and sexual counsel. And perhaps even more amazingly, this son seems to still respect his father, and desire his godly counsel.

Why do we incorrectly assume that Proverbs is addressing young children or teenagers? Because in our American culture, unlike many other cultures, only little kids are expected to listen to their parents. For 6 years I was at a Korean church, and it was eye-opening for me to see the respect that was shown to parents and elders. When you approached an older person, you bowed. Children didn't go to college or get married without his or her parents' approval. The average kid in America today could not care less what his or her parents think about his or her choice of college or spouse or "alternative lifestyle."

In the Hebrew culture, adult sons still had an obligation to listen to their fathers. Read the book of Genesis and you'll see that this is a given. This doesn't mean that fathers controlled their sons, but it does mean that fathers always had the right to instruct their sons, and we could even go so far as the say the obligation to instruct them. Another passage is prone to misunderstanding here, namely Genesis 2:24: "Therefore a man shall leave his father and mother and hold fast to his wife..." Yes, children are expected to establish their own households. But the application is not that parents can no longer counsel their children. Again, Proverbs 5:18 is a *married* son receiving counsel from his father.

What does the perfect Father and Son relationship look like? Something like this: "So Jesus said to them, 'When you have lifted up the Son of Man, then you will know that I am he, and that I do nothing on my own authority, but speak just as the Father taught me. And he who sent me is with me. He has not left me alone, for I always do the things that are pleasing to him'" (Jn. 8:28-29).

5

WALK WITH THE WISE

Practical Wisdom on Peer Pressure and Friendships

Genesis 2:18 is stunning. God Himself pronounces that something is not good in His perfect world. He says, '"It is not good that the man should be alone; I will make him a helper fit for him."' The immediate context of course is marriage, but the application is broader: God never created us to be alone. Technically speaking, Adam isn't alone. He has all the animals to relate to; even more significantly he has a relationship with the living God. Yet this isn't sufficient. At this point we are implicitly warned not to be more spiritual than God, and say, "All I need is God." That's simply not true. It wasn't even true before the fall, when Adam's relationship with God was unaffected by sin. We were created from the beginning with a need for a relationship with the living God *and* other people.

Proverbs 1:10 gives the first bit of practical advice to "my son." "My son, if sinners entice you, do not consent." These parents waste no time to pass along a warning about peer pressure. These parents clearly perceive the powerful influence of one's peers. I once heard about a man being interviewed on his 100th birthday. He was asked about the advantages of living so long. He quipped that he no longer had to worry about peer pressure. The rest of us do.

The Bible states that at every age we want godly, righteous, and wise friends. Therefore, we must choose our friends carefully. Proverbs 12:26 says, "A righteous man is cautious in friendship" (NIV). The English Standard Version footnote provides this possible translation of the difficult Hebrew, "The righteous chooses his friends carefully." The reason for this caution and careful choosing of friends is given in the second half of the verse: "but the way of the wicked leads them astray." It's an undeniable reality that our friends have a powerful influence upon us, in spite of our temptation to believe the contrary.

Pastor Steve Wilkins writes,

> "Young people especially need to understand and avoid this temptation, as they are more susceptible to surrounding influences, whether they realize it or not. Their friends will either provoke them to holiness or encourage them in wickedness—it will be one or the other. It is never neutral. God has so constituted us that we will become like our friends. It is folly for a young person to think that he will be the one who will turn around all of his foolish friends. There are far too many examples in Scripture against this kind of thinking for anyone to seriously believe it, but still, being sinners, we always like to make ourselves out as great heroes who will save everyone else in the end. The reality is that we are not great heroes, especially when we are young. And he will be another fool who fancies that he will be the exception. He tells himself that while everybody else is corrupted by bad friends, he will change them. He seems to ignore the fact that God has told him exactly the opposite. Over and over Scripture warns against ungodly companions."[12]

Proverbs is serious about admonishing us to avoid bad associations like the plague. We are to avoid violent men (1:15), those with perverted speech (2:12), fools (14:7), the proud (16:19), as well as a gossip who talks too much (29:19, NASB), and those who drink too much (23:20). Also, "Make no friendship with a man given to anger," and once again we are given the reason, "lest you learn his ways and entangle yourself in a snare" (22:24-25).

I want to remind young people, who are ready to assert their independence, that their friendships affect their parents. "A companion of gluttons shames his father" (28:7). Children who love God and their parents will be motivated to choose friends of whom their parents approve. Due to how God created us, friendships are inescapable, but we should continually evaluate whether our different friendships are a help or a hindrance to our Christian pilgrimage. If they really are a help it should be obvious to other people who are close to you, like your parents. Parents should be able to say to their son or daughter, "Since you've become friends with so-and-so, I've noticed that you've been more respectful" or "more disciplined with your homework" or "more concerned about honoring the LORD in all you do." If they say, "Since you've become friends with so-and-so, you've really had an attitude" or "you've become derelict in your chores" or "you've dressed more immodestly," then your friend clearly is a hindrance, no matter how much you may protest, or how popular the friend may be at school or in the neighborhood. There is no circumventing the immutable truth, "Whoever walks with the wise becomes wise, but the companion of fools will suffer harm" (13:20).

Do Not Be Unequally Yoked

The admonition "Do not be unequally yoked with unbelievers" (2 Cor. 6:14a) is a reference to a principle found in the

Old Testament originally concerning the yoking of different animals. The text Paul has in mind is Deuteronomy 22:10: '"You shall not plow with an ox and a donkey together."' Since these animals are so different, they shouldn't be expected to cooperate with each other in a close relationship.

It is worth noting that the animal kingdom is designed to teach us lessons about the Christian life. For example, we read in 1 Corinthians 9:9-10: "For it is written in the Law of Moses, 'You shall not muzzle an ox when it treads out the grain.' Is it for oxen that God is concerned? Does he not speak entirely for our sake? It was written for our sake, because the plowman should plow in hope and the thresher thresh in hope of sharing in the crop" (For other examples see Pro. 1:17; 6:5-8; 7:22). In addition to the application of the plowman and the thresher, Paul uses the principle about feeding oxen to show that there is a place for a minister to be paid for his spiritual work. Similarly, we are expected to say of Deuteronomy 22:10, "Is God concerned about the animals not cooperating with each other? Does he not speak entirely for our sake? It was written for our sake, because believers and unbelievers are so different that you shouldn't expect them to work well together in close, intimate relationships."

The question we are forced to ask in light of the admonition is "What kind of unions or relationships with unbelievers are prohibited?" Clearly, the separation Paul is calling for in this passage is not the separation of a monk who physically leaves the world to live in isolation in a mountain monastery where he only associates with other "holy people." Paul assumes that Christians will associate with sexually immoral people, greedy people, swindlers, and even idolaters (1 Cor. 5:9-10). Besides, without some kind of contact and interaction with pagans, we could never be the salt and light that Christ calls us to be (Matt. 5:13-16); we could never fulfill the Great Commission, which requires us to '"Go therefore and make disciples of all nations"' (Matt. 28:18-20)—nations that are wicked and sinful. However, it is also clear that Paul is concerned about the kinds of relationships that Christians have with non-Christians, and not all these relationship are OK. So, which are OK and which are not?

Murray Harris writes of being unequally yoked: "(T)his is a prohibition against forming *close attachments* with non-Christians… Paul is content to state a general principle that needs specific application under the Spirit's guidance. In expanded form the principle might be expressed thus: 'Do not form any relationship, whether temporary or permanent, with unbelievers that would lead to a compromise of Christian standards or jeopardize consistency of Christian witness. And why such separation? Because the unbeliever does not share the Christian's standards, sympathies, or goals."[13] The key idea here is that of "close attachments," and associations that result in compromise. And, unfortunately, this compromising happens more often than most Christians care to admit.

Second Corinthians 6:14 is often cited as Scriptural support to counsel a Christian not to marry a non-Christian. While this is a good application, which I wholeheartedly agree with, we need to realize that this is only one application of dozens that could be made. What about business partnerships? What about friendships? Many will respond, "But Jesus was a friend of sinners." Was he? Jesus' generation called him '"A glutton and a drunkard, a friend of tax collectors and sinners!"' (Lk. 7:34). But was any of that true? While Jesus dined with sinners, and declared the gospel to them, he wasn't technically their friend. Friendship with Jesus is conditional. Jesus said to his disciples, '"You are my friends if you do what I command you"' (Jn. 15:14). Only Christians can sincerely sing, "What a friend we have in Jesus…"

Five antithetical, rhetorical questions follow to reinforce the command to not be "unequally yoked." "For what partnership has righteousness with lawlessness? Or what fellowship has light with darkness? What accord has Christ with Belial? Or what portion does a believer share with an unbeliever? What agreement has the temple of God with idols?" (2 Cor. 6:14b-16a). The answer to each of these questions is an emphatic "NONE!" Christians and non-Christians may have much in common at a superficial level. But loving the same sports team is ultimately meaningless when you don't love and serve the same God. Consider carefully with whom you yoke.

Seek Godly Counsel from Elders, and Not Just Your Peers

I can still remember talking to one of my professors my senior year of college. I was young and eager to get into the ministry full-time, but he encouraged me to look at the big picture. His recommendation was that I seriously consider going to seminary and serving God with my master's degree and not just with my bachelor's. He told me I was young and single, so I should take advantage of that to get a few more years of education. From his perspective I had my whole life ahead of me, so I needed to build on a solid educational foundation. He was probably being polite, since he knew I wasn't ready for the ministry, and really needed a lot more training. Regardless, I praise God for bringing an older and wiser man into my life to provide me with godly counsel. It changed my life. Even as I write this my emotions are stirred at God's goodness. It's not an exaggeration to say that counsel can affect the whole trajectory of your life—positively or negatively, depending on the counsel.

Counsel can not only influence individual lives, it can also influence families, churches, and nations. Israel transitioned from being a united kingdom to being a divided kingdom, because Rehoboam, Solomon's son who succeeded him as king, rejected good counsel and followed bad counsel. First Kings 12 tells us that soon after Rehoboam became king, "Jeroboam and all the assembly of Israel came and said to Rehoboam, 'Your father made our yoke heavy. Now therefore lighten the hard service of your father and his heavy yoke on us, and we will serve you.' He said to them, 'Go away for three days, then come again to me'" (vv. 3-5). Rehoboam had better give a wise response, because it will determine the whole course of his reign over Israel. Rehoboam discerns this, so he seeks out counsel. Rehoboam is to be commended at this point. He at least has enough sense and humility to ask others what they think. "The way of a fool is right in his own eyes, but a wise man listens to advice" (Prov. 12:15). "(I)n an abundance of counselors there is safety" (11:14).

"Then King Rehoboam took counsel with the old men, who had stood before Solomon his father while he was yet alive, saying, 'How do you advise me to answer this people?' And they said to him, 'If you will be a servant to this people today and serve them, and speak good words to them when you answer them, then they will be your servants forever'" (1 Kgs. 12:6-7). Rehoboam has turned to his father's counselors for guidance. A prudent move, since these men have already proven to be reliable and capable men with years of experience under Solomon. They made it clear that a favorable answer would endear him to the people and would establish his throne securely.

"But [Rehoboam] abandoned the counsel that the old men gave him and took counsel with the young men who had grown up with him and stood before him… And the young men who had grown up with him said to him, 'Thus shall you speak to this people who said to you, "Your father made our yoke heavy, but you lighten it for us," thus shall you say to them, "My little finger is thicker than my father's thighs. And now, whereas my father laid on you a heavy yoke, I will add to your yoke. My father disciplined you with whips, but I will discipline you with scorpions…' So the king did not listen to the people, for it was a turn of affairs brought about by the LORD" (vv. 8, 10-11, 15). This harsh response resulted in a rebellion, with Rehoboam fleeing to Jerusalem, and Jeroboam becoming king over Israel. Thus the kingdom was divided. Only Judah followed Rehoboam (vv. 16-20). And the rest, as they say, is history.

I wish I could impress upon young people the importance of listening to those who are older and wiser. There is a reason why, for example, older women are to train the younger women to love their husband and children. The older women have learned a few things over the years that can benefit the next generation, if it will listen. Too many arrogant know-it-alls have unnecessarily made foolish decisions, because they thought they didn't need any outside input. I once talked with a Christian high school student who made a major life decision without talking to one mature Christian or even his parents who were Christians. The only counsel that came to this student was from unbelievers and other teenagers. As a general rule of thumb, the greater the decision, the greater the need for godly counsel, which usually means counsel from those who are older and have already been where you are. May our young people be different and heed the advice of Solomon: "Let the wise hear and increase in learning, and the one who understands obtain guidance" (Prov. 1:5).

6

Responding to Wisdom

The Consequences of Not Heeding the Voice of Wisdom

In Proverbs 1:20-33 wisdom is personified as a woman crying out to be heard. It's interesting that the author, Solomon, doesn't just present wisdom as a precept or a principle to be followed, but as a person to be obeyed. Who is this person? This person finds fulfillment in Christ.[14] Christ is the wisdom of God, as Proverbs 8 makes clear. Jesus Himself claimed to be wisdom or Truth incarnate (Jn. 14:6). When Pontius Pilate asked Jesus, "What is truth?" Jesus could have responded, "You're lookin' at it, buddy." I'm emphasizing this aspect of wisdom so we understand that to ignore or reject the voice of wisdom is to ignore or reject God Himself—this is personal.

Wisdom is eager to be heard. "Wisdom cries aloud in the street, in the markets she raises her voice; at the head of the noisy streets she cries out; at the entrance of the city gates she speaks" (Pro. 1:20-21). Markets are noisy places, due to all the commerce and commotion of the crowds. Therefore, if you wanted to be heard you had no choice but to raise your voice. So wisdom does, because she wants to be heard by *everyone*. To get into a walled city like Jerusalem you had to enter through the city gates. This is where wisdom positions herself so that she can be heard by all the people as they pass through the gates.

As the crowds pass through the gates wisdom cries aloud, '"How long, O simple ones, will you love being simple? How long will scoffers delight in their scoffing and fools hate knowledge?"' (vs. 22). The repeated "How long…How long?" indicates that wisdom is growing impatient. And do you know what the answer to the "How long?" question is? It is until they are ready to repent. Until that time they will continue to love being simple, to delight in scoffing, to hate knowledge—which is to say they will continue to mock God. But God is not mocked; a man reaps what he sows (Gal. 6:7).

You might be wondering, "Why would anybody hate knowledge?" The short answer is because the person is a fool, but the problem is not one of intelligence, it's one of morality. Fallen men have a profound distaste for knowledge about God and His truth, since it rebukes them, and admonishes them to leave behind their self-indulgent life of sin. Jesus of course was well aware of this. He said, "'And this is the judgment: the light has come into the world, and people loved the darkness rather than the light because their works were evil. For everyone who does wicked things hates the light and does not come to the light, lest his works should be exposed'" (Jn. 3:19-20).

Excuses, like claiming not to know whether or not God really exists, will not suffice on the Day of Judgment. Creation itself is a more than adequate testimony to God's eternal power and divine nature. The apostle Paul notes, "For his invisible attributes, namely, his eternal power and divine nature, have been clearly perceived, ever since the creation of the world, in the things that have been made. So they are without excuse" (Rom. 1:20). Paul goes on to tell how people respond to this revelation of God, who they really do know is out there (atheists are just those "who by their unrighteousness suppress the truth"—Rom. 1:18): "For although they knew God, they did not honor him as God or give thanks to him, but they became futile in their thinking, and their foolish hearts were darkened. Claiming to be wise, they became fools..." (vv. 21-22). Observe carefully how willful rejection of the truth about God affects one's heart and mind. This is the natural consequence (or supernatural consequence) of discarding the truth of God.

As if becoming a fool wasn't bad enough, God also gave them up "to do what ought not to be done" (vs. 28). Paul says, "Therefore God gave them up in the lusts of their hearts to impurity, to the dishonoring of their bodies among themselves, because they exchanged the truth about God for a lie and worshiped and served the creature rather than the Creator, who is blessed forever! Amen" (vv. 24-25). Exchanging the truth about God for a lie leads to sinful and wicked behavior. In case you missed the point, Paul basically repeats himself, using homosexuality as an example: "For this reason God gave them up to dishonorable passions. For their women exchanged natural relations for those that are contrary to nature; and the men likewise gave up natural relations with women and were consumed with passion for one another, men committing shameless acts with other men and receiving in themselves the due penalty for their error" (vv. 26-27). I hear Christians say, "God is going to judge homosexuals for their behavior." This is true, but it misses the point of Romans chapter 1, which is even more fundamental: Homosexuality, as well as other sins (see vv. 29-31), is itself the judgment of God (We'll deal with this a little further under the subheading *Under the Lord's Wrath*, in relation to Pro. 22:14).

Wisdom Can Bring Revival or Judgment, Life or Death

Wisdom says—if I can paraphrase—"How long will you fools continue to wallow in the muck and mire of your sin?" If the answer is *just a little longer*, be fully cognizant that judgment, which you are already under, could get even worse. You could go from darkness to even greater darkness. In 2 Thessalonians 2:10 Paul tells the believers about "those who are perishing, because they refused to love the truth and so be saved." He then continues, "Therefore God sends them a strong delusion, so that they may believe what is false, in order that all may be condemned who did not believe the truth but had pleasure in unrighteousness" (vv. 11-12).

Would God actually send a delusion to people for refusing to love the truth? He has in the past. The prophet Micaiah tells about his vision of heaven that would result in King Ahab's death: "I saw the Lord sitting on his throne, and all the host of heaven standing beside him on his right hand and on his left; and the Lord said, 'Who will entice Ahab, that he may go up and fall at Ramoth-gilead?' And one said one thing, and another said another. Then a spirit came forward and stood before the Lord, saying, 'I will entice him.' And the Lord said to him, 'By what means?' And he said, 'I will go out, and will be a lying spirit in the mouth of all his prophets.' And he said, 'You are to entice him, and you shall succeed; go out and do so'" (1 Kgs. 22:19-22). Sure enough, Ahab listened to the false prophets and was killed in battle. Responding to wisdom is not a game; God says in essence, "You don't want the truth? Fine, then I'll send you lies and delusions that will result in your own destruction."

Now let's look at the flip side. Wisdom promises, "'If you turn at my reproof, behold, I will pour out my spirit to you; I will make my words known to you'" (Pro. 1:23). This is nothing less than a promise for personal revival. If you respond to reproof with repentance, God will pour out His

Spirit and make His words known to you. I believe "spirit" should be spelled with a capital "S," because it seems to refer to the Holy Spirit. How is God's Word made known to us? Obviously it's through His Spirit. As I said, this is a reference to revival, which is seen in God promising not just to give us a little trickle of His Spirit, but to *pour out* His Spirit. This should remind us of the day of Pentecost in Acts 2 where Joel's prophecy was fulfilled and God poured out His Spirit. This is what is being promised in Proverbs. And corresponding to this is the promise of God to make His Word known to us. God's Spirit and God's Word work in tandem. Following the outpouring of the Spirit at Pentecost was an incredible response to the Word: "So those who received his word were baptized, and there were added that day about three thousand souls" (Acts 2:41).

Our hearts should leap when we hear wisdom say, "I will make my words known to you." I fear that too many of God's people aren't excited by this statement, because they fail to see how crucial the Word of God is to their lives. It's simple: When God wants to bless a people, He reveals His Word to them. Conversely, when He wants to curse a people, or judge them, there is a famine of hearing the words of God (Amos 8:11-12). Wisdom and truth are essential to the Christian life. If we want to live freely, that comes by the truth. Jesus said, "'If you abide in my word, you are truly my disciples, and you will know the truth, and the truth will set you free'" (Jn. 8:31-32). Do you want to grow in sanctification and Christ-likeness? Jesus prayed for His disciples, "'Sanctify them in the truth; your word is truth'" (Jn. 17:17). Martin Luther said, "The soul can do without all things except the Word of God," because he had no doubt about the blessings wrought by the Word.

However, always remember that the promise of wisdom cuts both ways. Wisdom also says, "'Because I have called and you refused to listen, have stretched out my hand and no one has heeded, because you have ignored all my counsel and would have none of my reproof, I also will laugh at your calamity; I will mock when terror strikes you'" (Pro. 1:24-26). This is not a jovial laugh; this is the laugh of vindication (similar to Ps. 2:4).

Imagine that the calamity has come. And it can come in a thousand different ways—a hurricane, a disease, a fire, a lost job. Wisdom warns us in advance, "'Then they will call upon me, but I will not answer; they will seek me diligently but will not find me. Because they hated knowledge and did not choose the fear of the LORD, would have none of my counsel and despised all my reproof, therefore they shall eat the fruit of their way'" (Pro. 1:28-31). Now, at last, these scoffers are ready to seek wisdom, but it's too late. Responding to wisdom is an urgent requirement. As the author of Hebrews wrote, "'Today, if you hear his voice, do not harden your hearts'" (Heb. 4:7).

Under the Lord's Wrath

In my devotional reading years ago, I was perplexed by this proverb: "The mouth of an adulteress is a deep pit; he who is under the LORD's wrath will fall into it" (Prov. 22:14, NIV). This peculiar proverb shows that responding to wisdom when facing a temptation is a little more complex than we may have thought at first.

The first half of this proverb is pretty straightforward. The mouth of the adulteress, most likely, refers to her kisses and seductive words (Prov. 7:5-27). By describing her mouth as a deep pit (see also Prov. 23:27) we are warned of the danger associated with her tantalizing kisses and words. There are consequences, which are extremely difficult to recover from for those enticed. It will not be easy to escape this pit—it is *deep*. This understanding is fairly obvious.

However, the way the second half of the proverb was linked to the first half made me stop and think. I expected the author to say something like: "He who falls into it *will* be under the LORD's wrath." The message, then, would be clear: "Beware of the adulteress, with her persuasive words, and stay as far away from her as you possibly can, because if she seduces you God will punish you." And this is precisely the message we find in many proverbs. "Keep your way far from her, and do not go near the door of her house… For a man's ways are before the eyes of the LORD, and he ponders all his paths" (Prov. 5:8, 21). "Do not desire her beauty in your heart, and do not let her capture you with her eyelashes; for the price of a prostitute is only a loaf of bread… So is he who goes in to his neighbor's wife; none who touches her will go unpunished" (Prov. 6:25-26, 29). This, however, is not the specific lesson of Proverbs 22:14.

When it comes to thinking about the wrath of God, this proverb causes us to take one or two chronological steps back from our usual way of thinking about God's wrath. For example, we all know that the Bible speaks of "the wrath to come" (1 Thess. 1:10). This wrath that was future for the Thessalonians (I believe it came in A.D. 70) encouraged godly living. Likewise, we should live in light of the final judgment (Rev. 20:11-15), but this is not the wrath described in our proverb.

There is also a wrath that takes place in this life. We come under the judgment of the Lord when we sin. Some of the Corinthians faced this judgment, when they partook of the Lord's Supper in an unworthy manner. "That is why," Paul told them, "many of you are weak and ill, and some have died" (1 Cor. 11:30). Paul went on to say, "But when we are judged by the Lord, we are disciplined so that we may not be condemned along with the world" (vs. 32). This is the wrath I expected to find in Proverbs 22:14, but didn't.

To understand the wrath of Proverbs 22:14, we must take one more step back, because it is a wrath that comes not only before the final wrath—but comes even before the wrath that is the result of sin in this life. It is the wrath that takes place prior to the sin, and, in fact, leads to the sin itself. It is a biblical and powerful truth that sin not only *leads* to the wrath of God, but also is the result of *already* being under the wrath of God. To paraphrase Matthew Henry, "It is the wrath of God leaving people to themselves to enter into temptation after He has removed the bridle of His restraining grace."

We see this wrath in Romans 1:18, which "is [present tense] revealed" against those who reject the truth about God, with the result being that "God gave them up" (this phrase is found three times, in Rom. 1:24, 26, 28) "in the lusts of their hearts…to dishonorable passions…to a debased mind." Similarly, the second half of Proverbs 22:14 reads, "he who is [presently] under the LORD's wrath will [when the temptation comes] fall into it." Sexual sin, itself, is evidence that a person was *already* under the LORD's wrath.

This same sequence is found in Ecclesiastes 7:26: "I find more bitter than death the woman who is a snare, whose heart is a trap and whose hands are chains. *The man who pleases God will escape her, but the sinner she will ensnare*" (NIV, emphasis added). If you escape, you prove that you were *already* pleasing God. If you are ensnared, you prove that you were *already* a sinner. To some extent, our responses to wisdom in the midst of temptation are determined before the temptation comes.

The implications here are staggering and a cause for great soul-searching. Many who are presently living in sin need to realize that God's wrath is not only farther down the road, but is also already upon them. The wrath of God described in our proverb is often overlooked, but it shouldn't be. It reminds us that we are in desperate need of the bridle of God's restraining grace every moment of every day.

7

Avoiding Adultery

Considering Defensive and Offensive Steps that Can Be Taken

Ask a person who has committed adultery, "How did it happen?" and you're likely to hear, "I don't know, it just happened." Adultery doesn't *just happen*—let's get real. It's not as though you're walking down the street, minding your own business, and then you accidentally step into a hole you didn't see, which causes you to fall to the ground in great pain and anguish. Then as you're lying there dazed and confused trying to recover, someone comes along and inquires, "What happened?" And you say with the world around you still spinning, "I'm not sure, it just happened." Adultery is not like that.

It's been said that adultery is not the result of a blowout, but of a slow leak. There is always a prelude to promiscuity. The purpose of Proverbs 2:1-19 (and several other passages in Proverbs) is to help us recognize that prelude, so we can be delivered from the forbidden woman (this also applies to the forbidden man, but Proverbs was written for boys, so the counsel is given to escape the forbidden woman).

Moreover, we must highlight the underlying presupposition, namely that men need to be delivered from the forbidden woman. The assumption is that young men (and older men) are vulnerable to this type of temptation. Therefore, our sons should be prepared in advance, so they will not be caught off guard by the snare of the seductress. Unfortunately, if we can trust the statistics, married women are now committing adultery nearly just as much as the men. This means adultery is an equal opportunity employer, so now both sexes require admonishing.

Proverbs provides us with preventive medicine. This is a tremendous aid, since the time to prepare for temptation is not after, but before it comes; before we destroy our marriages...our families...our reputations...our ministries. To prepare, let's meditate on three characteristics of the forbidden woman found in Proverbs 2:16-17: "So you will be delivered from the forbidden woman, from the adulteress with her smooth words [flattereth with her words, KJV], who forsakes the companion of her youth and forgets the covenant of her God." The three characteristics are flattering conversations, a forsaken companion, and a forgotten covenant.

First, we'll address flattering conversations. I'd like to set the stage by citing a list of warnings that exhort us to avoid adultery and the adulteress. "For her house sinks down to death, and her paths to the departed" (Pro. 2:18); "but in the end she is bitter as wormwood, sharp as a two-edged sword. Her feet go down to death; her steps follow the path to Sheol" (5:4-5); "none who go to her come back, nor do they regain the paths of life" (2:19); "He who commits adultery lacks sense; he who does it destroys himself" (6:32); "for many a victim has she laid low, and all her slain are a mighty throng. Her house is the way to Sheol [hell, KJV] going down to the chambers of death" (7:26-27).

Nancy Wilson asks: "Now given such manifold and dire warnings, whatever would possess a young man to turn aside to go after such a woman? What exactly is the pull? What is it that first lures him away to lust after her? Proverbs makes it very clear that the initial pull comes from flattery."[15]

The hook of adultery is baited with flattery. Yes, some men commit adultery for sheer sex—perhaps with a prostitute; but for the vast majority of Christian men, adultery begins with flattery. When the adulterer is lying in the ditch wondering how he got there, he will look back and see that he was involved in inappropriate and intimate conversations, which stroked his ego. This message is repeated in Proverbs. Proverbs has four "adultery passages" and all of them talk about the speech of the adulteress. "For the lips of a forbidden woman drip honey, and her speech is smoother than oil" (5:3; see also 6:24; 7:5). "With much seductive speech she persuades him…he does not know that it will cost him his life" (7:21, 23).

Nancy Wilson concludes that "young men in particular are very vulnerable to flattery. This must be connected to their God-given need for respect and admiration; so it follows that a man who does not feel respected for his legitimate attributes will be a sitting duck for flattery… So what is my point of application?... Wives: Respect your husband genuinely… Men who have a 'full tank' when it comes to respect from their wives are far less vulnerable to the flattery of the strange woman"[16] And husbands need to remember that women were created with a God-given desire for love. If a wife is secure in the love of her husband, and if he is sincerely honoring her as the weaker vessel, she will not feel the need to flirt or use flattery to get the attention of other men. Sometimes the best defense is a good offense.

The second characteristic of the adulteress, following flattering conversations, is a forsaken companion. How do we know she has forsaken the companion of her youth? Or, we could ask, "How can we recognize a straying wife?" Proverbs 7:10-12 gives us a couple of clues: "And behold, the woman meets him, dressed as a prostitute, wily of heart. She is loud and wayward; her feet do not stay at home; now in the street, now in the market, and at every corner she lies in wait." We have at least two indicators that this woman is straying from her husband, while he is away on a "long journey," perhaps for work (vs. 19). The first indicator is her dress—she dresses like a prostitute. Few things say, "Come and get it" to men more than immodest dress.

Immodest dress is so bad in America that even many unbelievers are disgusted with the clothing available for young women. I was listening to a talk show on a secular radio station one time as mother after mother called in complaining about how difficult it was for her to find appropriate attire for her daughter. I was listening to the program with my teenage daughter, and mentioned to her that you know it's bad when unbelievers are repulsed. The shorts are short shorts, the jeans are skin tight, the tops are just as tight and often don't cover the midsection much less other parts of a woman's anatomy. Just recently my son told me about a guy who wears girl pants. I asked, "What are girl pants?" I had never heard of "girl pants." He said, "Some guys buy and wear the girls' jeans that are super tight." He and his friends refer to them as girl pants. Just when you thought it couldn't get any worse, we descend down yet another step into the pit… (but I digress; now we're dealing with the women).

As a pastor, a father, and a man I want to exhort you young (and older) women to consider how you dress. Some of you are sending a message you don't want to send. Low-cut tops and high-cut skirts communicate looseness to men. You may not *intend* to send that message, you may not *want* to send that message, but nonetheless that is what men hear. Furthermore, if you ladies are praying for a godly Christian husband, you need to know that modesty is not only important to God (1 Tim. 2:9), it's also important to *Christian* men. I can still recall that just before two of my best friends got married, on different occasions, they both gave unsolicited comments about how they loved the fact that their wives-to-be dressed modestly. Immodesty may get a man's attention, but it will not gain his respect.

The second indicator that this woman is straying comes from her "loud and wayward" behavior—she's begging for attention and is going all over town to find it (Pro. 7:12). However, before we come down too hard on this woman, let's consider who her husband is. This woman says, "For my husband is not at home; he has gone on a long journey; he took a bag of money with him; at full moon he will come home" (vv. 19-20). Could it be that the forbidden woman is love-starved? Perhaps she's been neglected by her husband? The sad irony is that many men are away from home, working to make more money, so that the home can be a paradise, when their absence actually turns it into a lonely desert. We could write a new proverb: "Better is a little with close companionship, than a large castle full of luxuries... and loneliness."

Other husbands are consumed with hobbies or sports. I talked to a woman one time who said her husband played softball five nights a week. Hmm, I wonder why she wanted a divorce? And how many men are missing in action because they spend evening after evening lounging on a recliner with a beer in one hand and a TV remote in the other? Sorry, is this too meddlesome? Come on men, your wife needs a little bit of your undivided attention. But you're probably not even reading this, because the game is on; it's always on, isn't it? Maybe your wife will set this book in a strategic location, such as where she put the other Christian books on the family, that she was hoping and praying you would read, but didn't. Perhaps she'll have better luck this time.

For you who think the Bible isn't relevant or practical, read on. "Let your fountain be blessed [check a good commentary for the imagery], and rejoice in the wife of your youth, a lovely deer, a graceful doe. Let her breasts fill you at all times with delight; be intoxicated always in her love" (Pro. 5:18-19). As I said earlier, the Bible assumes we are vulnerable to sexual temptation, so God has provided us with an antidote—sexual satisfaction. God is not prudish or Victorian. In fact He commands husbands and wives not to deprive each other (1 Cor. 7:5). To overcome sexual temptation, usually what's needed is not more prayer or more Bible reading, but more physical intimacy.

After flattering conversations and a forsaken companion, the third characteristic of the adulteress is that of a forgotten covenant. "[She] forgets the covenant of her God" (Pro. 2:17). There are two possible interpretations for "the *covenant* of her God." This could refer to the marriage covenant. The adulteress woman is breaking the covenant she made before God on the day she got married, when she promised her husband that she would leave all others, and keep herself only unto him.

The other possibility, which I lean toward, is that the covenant represents her relationship with God. We tend to talk about a personal relationship with God through Jesus Christ, which is OK, but in both the Old Testament and the New Testament this relationship is expressed in terms of being in covenant with God.

When Jesus instituted the Lord's Supper, He said, "'This cup is the new covenant in my blood. Do this, as often as you drink it, in remembrance of me'" (1 Cor. 11:25). The New Covenant is a reference to Jeremiah 31:31-34: "Behold, the days are coming, declares the Lord, when I will make a new covenant with the house of Israel and the house of Judah…this is the covenant that I will make with the house of Israel after those days, declares the Lord: I will put my law within them, and I will write it on their hearts. And I will be their God, and they shall be my people… For I will forgive their iniquity, and I will remember their sin no more."

God's people have always been in a relationship with God through covenants, culminating in the New Covenant. If this is the interpretation of "the covenant of her God," the application is that we avoid adultery by maintaining an ongoing, intimate relationship with our God and Savior.

And, I want to stress that this covenantal relationship includes learning sound doctrine (i.e., theology). Too many Christians think that more learning doesn't have any connection with being a more loving Christian, or a more loving spouse, or a more faithful spouse, but it does. Yes, knowledge can puff up and love is the greatest of all the virtues, yet love flourishes in knowledge, not ignorance (see Phil. 1:9). Orthodoxy (right doctrine) and orthopraxy (right practice) go hand in hand. Put bluntly, stupid Christians who don't know their Bibles are the ones lacking in love, and the ones vulnerable to adultery.

In this study of "avoiding adultery" we've been focusing on Proverbs 2:16-17: "So you will be delivered from the forbidden woman..." But notice that verse 16 begins with the word "So," which means that it is connected to the previous verses (1-15). The chapter begins, "My son, if you receive my words and treasure up my commandments with you, making your ear attentive to wisdom and inclining your heart to understanding...then you will understand the fear of the Lord and find the knowledge of God...he stores up sound wisdom for the upright; he is a shield to those who walk in integrity...discretion will watch over you, understanding will guard you, delivering you from the way of evil... *So you will be delivered from the forbidden woman...*" The flow here is important: This father is instructing his son with sound doctrine, and exhorting him to seek wisdom, so that he will fear God and find the knowledge of God, in order to walk in integrity and be delivered from evil, which includes being delivered from the forbidden woman. Practically, we teach our sons about God when they are 5 years old, so they will not be immoral when they are 15 or 25. A man with a vibrant, doctrinally-sound, covenantal relationship with God is not as likely to be seduced by the forbidden woman as is the ignorant Christian, who has not moved beyond Christianity 101 truths.

John Piper writes that the average evangelical doesn't live substantially differently from his unbelieving neighbor. However, "(f)or those who belittle doctrine as troublesome, it may come as a surprise that [Christians with a biblical worldview, as opposed to Christians without one, do live] differently from the world." Piper adds, "Ronald Sider, in his new book, *The Scandal of the Evangelical Conscience*, describes the difference: '[According to Barna Group statistics,] (t)hey are 9 times more likely than all the others to avoid "adult-only" material on the Internet. They are...twice as likely to choose not to watch a movie specifically because of its bad content...twice as likely to volunteer time to help needy people.'" Piper cites more of Sider's statistics, but Sider's conclusion, quoted by Piper, is crucial: '"[These] findings on the different behavior of Christians with a biblical worldview underline the importance of theology. Biblical orthodoxy does matter. One important way to end the scandal of contemporary Christian behavior [including adultery] is to work and pray fervently for the growth of orthodox theological belief in our churches."'[17]

8

Slow to Anger

A Look at Anger that Is a Reflection of God Himself

Not all expressions of anger are wrong or out of line. The antithesis in Proverbs is not between getting angry and not getting angry; rather the antithesis—and we must always put it in the right place—is between being slow to anger and being quick to anger. "Whoever is slow to anger has great understanding, but he who has a hasty temper exalts folly" (Pro. 14:29). "A hot-tempered man stirs up strife, but he who is slow to anger quiets contention" (15:18). We are exhorted to be slow to anger, which means we are to be like our God, who is often described as being slow to anger.

When the Lord appeared to Moses, part of that revelation included the truth that God is "slow to anger" (Ex. 34:6). Nahum delivered an oracle concerning judgment upon Nineveh, including a reminder that "The Lord is slow to anger and great in power, and the Lord will by no means clear the guilty. His way is in whirlwind and storm, and the clouds are the dust of his feet…The mountains quake before him; the hills melt; the earth heaves before him, the world and all who dwell in it. Who can stand before his indignation? Who can endure the heat of his anger? His wrath is poured out like fire, and the rocks are broken into pieces by him" (Nah. 1:3, 5-6). Yes, God is slow to anger, but nonetheless He does get angry. There's no getting around this aspect of God's character. In fact, "God is angry with the wicked every day" (Ps. 7:11, KJV).

Too many Christians insist that these passages don't apply, because they describe the God of the Old Testament. My response is, "So what?" The God of the Old Testament is the same God that we find in the New Testament. "Jesus Christ is the same yesterday and today and forever" (Heb. 13:8). It's not as though God has mellowed over time. Do we think that during the Old Testament era sin angered God, but now in the New Testament era God isn't bothered by murder, rape, idolatry, theft, etc.?

Let's not forget that there were times when Jesus, who is gentle and lowly in heart, got angry (see Mk. 3:1-6; 11:15-17; Matt. 23); likewise, let us not forget that Christians in the New Testament era were on occasion put to death for their sin (e.g., Ananias and Sapphira in Acts 5:1-11, as well as some of the Corinthians who were not discerning the body during Communion, and consequently they ate and drank judgment on themselves [1 Cor. 11:29-30]). God is *slow* to anger; He doesn't fly off the handle at the least little peccadillo, but He does get angry and He does unleash His wrath. And we certainly don't want to presume to know how God may or may not express His anger.

As evangelicals, we talk about the need to "be saved" all the time. Well, what exactly do we need to be saved from? The devil? In one sense we do, since he takes captives to do his will (Eph. 2:1-2; 2 Tim. 2:26). But in the ultimate sense, we need to be saved from the wrath of God—hell. Therefore, His anger should provoke our greatest fear, since He can destroy both soul and body in hell (Matt. 10:28).

God gets angry, but He never sins. We are to imitate Him. In Ephesians 4:26, Paul writes, "Be angry and do not sin." "Be angry" is a present passive imperative verb, which means it's a command. God commands His people to be angry. I wonder how many Christians think of anger as a fruit of the Spirit? We need to tread carefully here, since "*fits* of anger" are a work of the flesh (Gal. 5:20). But with that being said, there is a place for righteous indignation. For example, In 1 Samuel 11, the Ammonites have besieged Jabesh-gilead. In response the men of Jabesh want to make a treaty with the Ammonites, but the Ammonites will do so only if the Israelites allow them to gouge out all the Israelites' right eyes and thus bring disgrace on all Israel. When Saul hears about this, we read, "And the Spirit of God rushed upon Saul when he heard these words, and his anger was greatly kindled" (vs. 6). And then Saul put together an army and routed the enemy. We're not accustomed to thinking this way, due to our overreaction to the damage anger can cause, but righteous indignation is a fruit of the Spirit.

Martin Luther said that he never preached or prayed so well as when he was angry. One of the problems with modern evangelicals is that they're not disturbed enough by sin. Our calm composure in the face of horrific wickedness is not a virtue, but a vice; that which angers God causes us no concern at all. Evil and corruption and injustice and perversity, which once upon a time enraged the people of God, now only get a shrug of the shoulders and a yawn. We need to repent, and ask God to forgive us for not being slow to anger. Let me reiterate—we don't want to be hotheads, but we need to recognize that there's a place for Christ-like anger.

Practical Commands to Help Us Not Sin in Our Anger

A number of years ago I was stunned by a survey taken among youth pastors who said the second greatest problem they deal with in their ministries among junior and senior high school students is anger. I remember thinking, "Kids today are really mad, and getting madder." But let's be honest, so are many adults. "Road rage" and "going postal" are just two terms that have been coined in my lifetime to describe some of the fury and violence all around us. The fact that we get angry is not surprising to me, but what is surprising to me is the increasing levels of anger that seem to be prevalent in our culture.

James counsels, "Know this, my beloved brothers: let every person be quick to hear, slow to speak, slow to anger; *for the anger of man does not produce the righteousness that God requires*" (Jam. 1:19-20, NIV, emphasis added). I've thought about these verses a fair amount, because I get angry too, and need to be reminded that my quick, uncontrolled anger is not the tool God will use to bring about the righteousness He requires.

James gives us four practical commands to help us not sin in our anger and help bring about the righteousness that God requires.

First, *be quick to hear*. Good listening is a lost art. Dr. Paul Tournier, the late Swiss Christian physician/therapist, said, "Listen to all the conversations of our world, between nations as well as those between couples. They are, for the most part, *dialogues of the deaf*." All of us, I'm sure, have been involved in conversations where vacant or wandering eyes indicated that our words were not landing. They were like an airplane caught in a holding pattern; they kept circling the runway, but never landed.

In my estimation, the best thing I learned in my pastoral counseling class in seminary was the importance of attentive listening. I decided to conduct "a listening experiment." I made a concerted effort to listen well, which I still did not do all that well, but I discovered that focused listening does make a difference. Most people just long to have somebody's undivided attention. And when we make a concerted effort to listen to others before reacting, it keeps anger in check.

Second, *be slow to speak*. This is James' way of saying, "Use a little common sense and think before you speak." Zeno, the Stoic Greek philosopher said, "We have two ears and one mouth, therefore we should listen twice as much as we speak." If you've ever opened your mouth only to change the foot within it, you understand the importance of being slow to speak. Keep in mind: You never have to take back what you didn't say. A friend of mine from college was fond of saying, "Make your words sweet, because you may have to eat them some day."

Jesus warned us, "'I tell you, on the day of judgment people will give account for every careless word they speak'" (Matt. 12:36). Therefore, it is incumbent upon us to weigh every word carefully.

Third, *be slow to anger*. There is a logical connection between being quick to hear, slow to speak, and slow to anger. Douglas Moo wrote, "Significantly, looseness in speech is often linked with unrestrained anger."[18] We also see this connection in Proverbs 17:27: "Whoever restrains his words has knowledge, and he who has a cool spirit is a man of understanding." If you can control your tongue, you can most likely control your temper. In fact, if you can control your tongue, James says you can control your whole body: "(I)f anyone does not stumble in what he says, he is a perfect man, able also to bridle his whole body" (Jam. 3:2).

How should we respond if we are on the receiving end of anger? Proverbs 15:1 gives us great counsel: "A soft answer turns away wrath, but a harsh word stirs up anger." Anger rarely makes a situation better, but it frequently makes it worse, "for the anger of man does not produce the righteousness that God requires."

Finally, *receive the implanted word*. "Therefore put away all filthiness and rampant wickedness and receive with meekness the implanted word, which is able to save your souls" (Jam. 1:21). There is no way that we will produce the righteousness that God requires apart from His Word. If you've been neglecting Bible reading and Bible study, you are not growing in righteousness—it's that simple. D.L. Moody said, "Sin will keep you from this Book, or this Book will keep you from sin." It's either one way or the other. If you are a Christian the Word is already implanted; but will it now grow because the soil of your soul is regularly being cultivated by humble acceptance?

If there is any doubt about what it means to "receive with meekness the implanted word," verse 22 will make it crystal clear: "But be doers of the word, and not hearers only, deceiving yourselves."

More Considerations on How to Eliminate Anger from the Body of Christ

"Be angry and do not sin; do not let the sun go down on your anger" (Eph. 4:26). The Bible assumes that all of us will get angry—some of us more than others. The evidence of this anger is everywhere. A number of people will be murdered before this day is over, due to anger. In addition to this, wives will be beaten and children will be abused, because of uncontrollable rage. Angry words will wound, unnecessarily sabotaging marriages, ministries, and close relationships.

Not only does our anger hurt others, but it also hurts us. Studies exploring the linkage between psychological and physiological conditions are discovering that obsession with vengeance may be a cause of such a diverse array of ailments as arthritis, asthma, headaches, allergic disorders, ulcers, high blood pressure and heart attacks, just to name a few. We could state it this way: "Anger eats its own container." Anger is a devastating force, and its con-sequences are sickening in more ways than one.

While anger is inevitable, God's Word is also plain that anger doesn't have to lead to sin—indeed it shouldn't lead to sin. "Be angry *and do not sin.*" How should we respond when we're angry? First, due to our wrong responses to anger, let me mention a couple of ways in which we shouldn't respond.

To begin with, we shouldn't fully express and vent our anger. Some psychologists have advocated dispensing of anger by indiscriminately unloading it. The theory is if you keep it bottled up inside, you will eventually explode, so you must release it before it becomes really destructive. Therefore, some counselors have advised that if a child is angry, toward say a parent for example, you might try giving the child a teddy bear and telling him or her to pretend that it's Mom or Dad and to punch it instead of the parent. This is supposed to release the anger like a valve on an overinflated tire, without actually hurting the parent. This psychobabble is not wise counsel. The Bible says, "A fool gives full vent to his anger, but a wise man keeps himself under control" (Prov. 29:11, NIV). The false presupposition is that expressing anger removes it. Venting anger doesn't eliminate anger, but actually *intensifies* anger. Venting is like any sin. Acting on it only allows you to give in more easily next time. I even hear Christians thanking other Christians for letting them "vent." We seem to think that spewing forth a list of grievances is a God-appointed means for building up the body of Christ. This is a sad indication that our thinking is more worldly than biblical.

We are not to fully express our anger, nor are we to fully suppress our anger. When an injustice leaves us angry, God doesn't tell us to ignore it or suppress it. God is angered by sin, so, as we said earlier, it isn't wrong for us to be *slow* to anger when we encounter unrighteousness, injustice, wickedness, etc. However, if the issues that caused our anger are not dealt with, anger and bitterness can accumulate over time. I've had people mad at me for things that I did one, two, or even three years before. On more than one occasion

I've said, "If this bothered you so much why didn't you say something to me?" Obviously, they were afraid to, and they allowed their anger to fester. Ephesians tells us to not let the sun go down on our anger.

Dealing with anger can be tricky, since anger isn't always black and white; a lot of anger is gray. If we're honest with ourselves we know that while some of our anger could be called "righteous indignation," we also have additional anger mingled in that is the result of our egos being bruised or our selfish desires going unfulfilled. Thus, part of our anger is justified, and part of it isn't. But how are we to deal with anger that is basically justified? Two answers will at least give us a good start. First, much anger, if not most, probably needs to be released by forgiving the person who has wronged us without a word said to anybody except God. Paul counsels Christians, "Bear with each other and forgive whatever grievances you may have against one another. Forgive as the Lord forgave you" (Col. 3:13, NIV).

If we can't let a grievance go, for whatever reason, the Bible tells us what we should do: "If your brother sins against you, go and tell him his fault, between you and him alone. If he listens to you, you have gained your brother. But if he does not listen, take one or two others along with you… If he refuses to listen to them, tell it to the church. And if he refuses to listen even to the church, let him be to you as a Gentile and a tax collector" (Matt. 18:15-17). If this process is followed there is no reason to get angry, because, at least in a biblically functioning church, there will eventually be resolution—be it reconciliation or discipline.

9

ELIMINATING ENVY

One Way Is by Fighting Fire with Fire

The apostle Paul tells us about the importance of contentment: "Now there is great gain in godliness with contentment, for we brought nothing into the world, and we cannot take anything out of the world. But if we have food and clothing, with these we will be content" (1 Tim. 6:6-8).

I'm sure you're often content (I'll believe the best), but what happens, ladies, when your good friend Sally gets a new outfit? All of a sudden yours by comparison looks tattered and…well…looks just blah. Or consider your old beat-up pick up truck, guys. That Ford's been more faithful to you than a dog. But last week you noticed a new luxury sedan in your neighbor's driveway, and by comparison your Ford just doesn't measure up any longer. Or you could think about your kid's toys. My kids have so many toys they could probably play with a different toy every day for a year. However, if they go over to a friend's house, and their friend may have only two toys in the whole house, but if they're two toys that my kids don't have they will feel that their mountain of toys is deficient. Why is this? Envy, pure and simple.

In the U.S. alone, advertisers spend $6 billion *a day* to make adults and children envious. It's funny (or maybe not so funny) to watch children come running to their parents after they see a commercial, and now they're just dying to have a toy they didn't even know existed two minutes ago. Before we laugh, let's remember that we adults are not much more mature at times. But we can't blame our envy on the advertising industry. If all advertising were to cease tomorrow, envy would still continue to be a problem, because it's a problem of the heart.

Solomon wrote, "Then I saw that all toil and all skill in work come from a man's envy of his neighbor" (Eccl. 4:4a). This is an overstatement of course, but it is meant to challenge us, to provoke us to ask, "Why am I doing what I'm doing?" "Am I really working for the glory of God, and to provide appropriately for my family, or, if the truth were known, am I often driven by envy?" The late American newspaper editor Emile Henry Gauvreau described himself with painful honesty as being "part of that strange race of people aptly described as spending their lives doing things they detest, to make money they don't want, to buy things they don't need, to impress people they dislike." And let me add that ministers of the Gospel are not immune. "Some indeed preach Christ from envy and rivalry, but others from good will" (Phil. 1:15).

Proverbs 3:31 warns us about the effect of envy: "Do not envy a man of violence and do not choose any of his ways." While there may be two separate commands here, I believe the commands are related this way: Do not envy a man of violence, because if you do you will be enticed to imitate his behavior. The application of this verse doesn't need to be limited to a man of violence. It also applies to envy of a man of power or greed or lust or dishonesty, etc. Envy may *begin* by desiring another person's position or popularity or possessions, but it *ends* with living as that person lives—or trying to, at least.

As an example, let's say a teenager watches MTV, and the show is about Britney Spears' crib (slang for house). If you envy her luxurious mansion, the temptation will be to "choose her ways," which could mean dressing like a sleaze. All across America girls are baring their midriffs like Britney Spears due to envy; even if most of the time they're not aware of why they're doing what they're doing. Now some equal time for the guys. Why are they wearing baggy pants, so that literally half their underwear is showing, making you wonder how their pants stay up? Why are they dressing like this? Did someone dare them to dress like this? Did someone pay them to dress like this? No, they did it of their own volition, because they envy the rap singers who dress like this. They envy the rappers' popularity or money or groupies or whatever, and once again the end result is that they "choose their ways."

The good news is that the principle of Proverbs 3:31 can be stated positively as well. We might say, "Admire a man of righteousness and choose his ways." This is why we should read Christian biographies. I'm still inspired by the faith of Betsie ten Boom exhibited in a Nazi concentration camp, and the courage and conviction of Stonewall Jackson during the Civil War. It is also one reason why the Bible is full of inspiring men and women, such as Noah, Abraham, Joseph, David, Daniel, Ruth, Esther, *et al.* You could look at it this way: As parents we're fighting fire with fire. Our children are going to be envious, but instead of being envious of the rich and famous who have little or no moral standards, why not place moral and spiritual giants in their paths through the Bible, good books, and good movies, so that they will admire (a positive form of envy) a man of righteousness and "choose his ways." It's inevitable that our kids will have heroes; let's just pray to God that they are the right ones.

Envy Is More than a Harmless Peccadillo

"Let not your heart envy sinners, but continue in the fear of the LORD all the day" (Pro. 23:17). Our tendency is to view envy as a relatively harmless peccadillo. Yes, we admit that it's a sin—the Bible makes that clear enough—but is a little envy of what my neighbor has, like a nicer car for example, really that serious? Aren't there other sins, we wonder, that we should be more concerned about? Maybe, maybe not.

Psalm 73 is an autobiographical psalm by Asaph. In this psalm he honestly describes his struggle with envy, and how it almost destroyed his soul, in addition to his emotional well-being. Asaph admitted, "Truly God is good to Israel, to those who are pure in heart. But as for me, my feet had almost stumbled, my steps had nearly slipped. For I was envious of the arrogant when I saw the prosperity of the wicked" (Ps. 73:1-3). Asaph is confessing that he almost became an apostate, due to envy. For Asaph, at least, envy didn't prove to be a harmless peccadillo; on the contrary it had the potential to be a damning sin.

Consider four effects that envy had upon Asaph, which are recorded in this psalm for our instruction. These effects—what Asaph experienced—can be applied to the envious generally. First, those who are envious struggle to believe in the goodness of God. Or they may believe that God is good, just not toward them. This may seem like a little thing, but who is going to devote his or her life to a mean or an unjust god? It is crucial to "taste and see that the LORD is good!" (Ps. 34:8). If a person doubts the goodness of God, the person's spiritual life can only spiral down from there.

Second, the envious have difficulty perceiving the truth of reality. In verses 4-12 Asaph describes *his* perspective of the wicked, whom he envied: "For they have no pangs until death; their bodies are fat and sleek. They are not in trouble as others are; they are not stricken like the rest of mankind"

(vv. 4-5). He concluded, "Behold, these are the wicked; always at ease, they increase in riches" (vs. 12). Is this true? Do the wicked have no pangs or trouble like the rest of us have? Are they *always* at ease? Do they *never* struggle? Do their investments only yield ever-increasing wealth? Hardly, but envy distorts your view of reality.

Third, the envious have trouble persevering in holiness. At one point Asaph believed, "All in vain have I kept my heart clean and washed my hands in innocence" (vs. 13). "What's the use?" Asaph was thinking. He's on the verge of throwing in the spiritual towel.

Fourth, the envious person sees his glass as half empty, while his neighbor's is half full. The result is bitter anguish: "For all the day long I have been stricken and rebuked every morning" (vs. 14). Socrates was right: "The envious are pained by their friends' successes." We could add: Or anybody else's success for that matter.

An envious person cannot be happy if others have more than he or she does, which is a huge problem, because somebody will always have more. There's an old tale about a greedy man and an envious man who were walking together in perfect harmony. That is until a genie appeared to them one day and said, "I will grant one of you one wish—with one condition. What ever you ask for the other man will receive double." The greedy man wasn't about to go first, because his greed wouldn't let him. The envious man also didn't want to make the wish, because he couldn't stomach the thought of his friend having twice as much as he had. They were at a standstill, and then the envious man finally said, "I wish to be blind in one eye."

This envious spirit is the opposite of love. "(L)ove does not envy" (1 Cor. 13:4). Since John the Baptist loved Christ so much, he was never envious, even though some of his disciples were: "And they came to John and said to him, 'Rabbi, he who was with you across the Jordan, to whom you bore witness—look, he is baptizing, and all are going to him.' John answered, 'A person cannot receive even one thing unless it is given him from heaven.'" (Jn. 3:26-27). The Pharisees, however, manifested a very different spirit toward Jesus' growing popularity. As a result of the testimony of the crowd that had been with Jesus when He raised Lazarus from the dead, many were flocking to Jesus. "So the Pharisees said to one another, 'You see that you are gaining nothing. Look, the world has gone after him'" (Jn. 12:19). Consequently, the religious leaders did everything in their power to have Christ crucified. Pilate might have been a coward, but he wasn't fooled by the religious leaders. Mark notes in his Gospel, "For he perceived that it was out of envy that the chief priests had delivered him up" (Mk. 15:10). Envy will not rest until its enemies are destroyed. And if envy isn't eliminated from our lives it will result in our own eternal destruction—"because those given over to envy…will not inherit the kingdom of God" (Gal. 5:21).

A Few More Simple Suggestions for Eliminating Envy

Paul addresses this issue of envy head-on: "Let us not become conceited, provoking one another, envying one another" (Gal. 5:26).

How can we eliminate envy from our lives? Prayer is a good place to begin. Pray for God to change your spirit and—this will be more difficult to do—pray for those you envy. Don't pray for their downfall, but for their success. F.B. Meyer was pastor of Christ Church in London at the same time that G. Campbell Morgan was pastor of Westminster Chapel and Charles H. Spurgeon was pastor of the Metropolitan Tabernacle. Both Morgan and Spurgeon often had much larger congregations than did Meyer. Meyer was troubled by envy. He later confessed that he didn't have peace of heart until he began praying for his colleagues.

"When I prayed for their success," Meyer said, "the result was that God filled their churches so full that the overflow filled mine, and it has been full since." Is there anybody in your life you should pray for? Keep in mind that the goal is not just to be thankful for what God has given you, but also for what God has given others. The envious cannot "rejoice with those who rejoice" (Rom. 12:15).

Also, we should stop comparing ourselves to others. This can only result in frustration or pride. We all have different spiritual gifts and different roles to play in the body of Christ. After Jesus rose from the dead he told Peter "by what kind of death he was to glorify God" and then He said, '"Follow me"' (Jn. 21:19). Peter then saw John out of the corner of his eye and said, '"Lord, what about this man?"' (vs. 21). Jesus responded, '"If it is my will that he remain until I come, what is that to you? You follow me!"' (vs. 22). Our vocation is to follow Christ and do what He is calling us to do. When we ask, "What about so-and-so?" we will only find ourselves distracted and side tracked from what God wants from us. Jesus' words need to be heard loud and clear, "What is that to you? You follow me!"

Envy will cease to be a problem when we can accept God's providence for our lives. This, in part at least, kept John the Baptist from being envious of Jesus' success. He said, '"A person cannot receive even one thing unless it is given him from heaven"' (Jn. 3:27).

Furthermore, the truth is that we often envy people we ought to pity. In the literature of ancient China is a story that demonstrates how foolish envy really is. There once was a wise man who had many wonderful horses. One horse in particular was so strong, fast, and beautiful that it elicited the envy of the man's neighbor. However, one day this horse escaped from the barn and ran away into the hills. The neighbor's envy changed to pity, but the wise man said, "Who knows if I should be pitied or if I should be envied because of this?"

The next day the horse returned to the wise man, leading a herd of 50 equally beautiful wild horses with him. The neighbor once again was filled with envy, and once again the wise man said, "Who knows if I should be envied or if I should be pitied because of this?" Shortly after the wise man said this, his only son tried to ride one of the wild horses, fell off of it, and broke his right leg. The neighbor's envy once again turned to pity, but the wise man responded by saying, "Who knows if I should be pitied or if I should be envied because of this?"

The next day the general of the emperor's army came to draft the wise man's son for an exceedingly dangerous mission, but since the son's leg was broken, he could not be recruited for this mission that promised certain death. The neighbor, whose own son was taken in the place of the injured young man, envied the wise man; and once again the wise man said, "Who knows if I should be envied or if I should be pitied because of this?" The story goes on and on with similar twists that shift the neighbor's feelings from envy to pity and then back to envy. The moral of the story is obvious: Too often our judgments are narrow, premature, and just plain wrong.

Asaph was cured of his envy when he went into the sanctuary of God and discerned the end of the wicked. He became aware that God sets them in slippery places and that they are destroyed in a moment (Ps. 73:17-19). Only a fool would envy a wealthy pagan when hell awaits the pagan at the end of the road.

Finally, remember that nothing compares to Christ. When Asaph stopped thinking like an ignorant, brute beast and could reason coherently once again, he saw that he actually had everything that heaven and earth could offer in his Lord. Asaph exulted, "Whom have I in heaven but you? And there is nothing on earth that I desire besides you" (Ps. 73:25). As Christians, we have found the hidden treasure; we possess the pearl of great value; we are heirs of the kingdom. So why would we envy those possessing fool's gold and plastic trinkets?

10

REWARDS FOR RIGHTEOUSNESS

And They Are Not All Spiritual

The introduction to the book of Proverbs makes it clear that one of its main purposes is to instruct God's people "in righteousness" (Pro. 1:3). For clarification, the righteousness addressed here is not objective or positional righteousness, but practical righteousness. In other words, we're dealing with sanctification, and not justification (although this is not to suggest that the two are unrelated).

For starters, we need to remember that "To do righteousness and justice is more acceptable to the LORD than sacrifice" (21:3). Because we aren't doing righteousness, our country, the United States, is—to borrow a phrase from Robert H. Bork—slouching towards Gomorrah. And don't forget about the judgment that fell upon that wicked city. Proverbs says, "Righteousness exalts a nation, but sin is a reproach to any people." *Righteousness* exalts a nation, not tolerance, not diversity, not the power of the military, not the strength of the economy, not health care, and not even lower prices at the gas pump. Democrats, Libertarians, Independents, and Republicans alike must see that the need of the hour is righteousness—as God defines it.

Let's not be ambiguous as to how righteousness will flourish in this nation, and in others. I fear that even Christian parents don't grasp what is needed to produce righteous living in our young people. For example, it's obvious that sexual immorality among teenagers is an epidemic. The solution advocated by those on the left, such as Planned Parenthood, is the liberal distribution of prophylactics, and providing abortion on demand—usually without parental consent. Those on the right react, and say we need to teach abstinence. When an abstinence program is welcomed by a school, we jump up and down, and shout, "Hip, hip, hooray!" While teaching abstinence is certainly better than tossing out condoms like candy at a 4th of July parade, we need to ask an honest, pragmatic question: "Does it really work?" I hate to be the bearer of bad news, but it doesn't. A recent study revealed that of 12,000 teenagers who took pledges to wait until marriage to have sex, 80% had sex outside of marriage in the following seven years.

Colossians 2:21-23 should have taught us a long time ago that this approach wouldn't go very far: "'Do not handle, Do not taste, Do not touch'...These have indeed an appearance of wisdom in promoting self-made religion and asceticism and severity to the body, but they are of no value in stopping the indulgence of the flesh." It's going to take more than bumper sticker slogans like "Just Say No" to curb the behavior of this promiscuous generation. Paul is clear: Rules alone are of no value in stopping the indulgence of the flesh.

So what will bring righteousness to our nation, and to our young people? NOTHING...except the transforming gospel of Jesus Christ. Paul said, "For I am not ashamed of the gospel, for it is the power of God for salvation to everyone who believes, to the Jew first and also to the Greek. For in it the righteousness of God is revealed from faith for faith, as it is written, 'The righteous shall live by faith'" (Rom. 1:16-17). What produces righteousness is not moralism or human effort, but the grace of God. Paul writes, "For the grace of God that brings salvation has appeared to all men. It teaches us to say 'No' to ungodliness and worldly passions, and to live self-controlled, upright and godly lives in this present age" (Titus 2:11-12). It's idealistic foolishness to think that people will "Just Say No" apart from the grace of God.

One of the purposes of the Law, with commands such as "Thou shalt not kill, Thou shalt not commit adultery, Thou shalt not steal, etc.," was to show us our sin, and our *inability* to "Just Say No." The Law highlights our utter dependence upon the grace of God to do righteousness. Now "sin will have no dominion over you," Paul says, "since you are not under law but under grace" (Rom. 6:14). And contrary to what some think, grace doesn't nullify the law (for example, the Ten Commandments still apply); rather it empowers us to fulfill the law. Righteousness is so important to God that He sent His one and only Son to die, in order to make it a reality in our lives. Peter makes this plain: "He himself bore our sins in his body on the tree, that we might die to sin and live to righteousness" (1 Pet. 2:24).

Now I'd like us to consider some rewards for righteousness that Proverbs mentions. And of course these Proverbs are designed to encourage and promote righteousness among the people of God. For starters, there is a reference to general blessings. "The LORD's curse is on the house of the wicked, but he blesses the dwelling of the righteous" (Pro. 3:33). "Blessings are on the head of the righteous, but the mouth of the wicked conceals violence" (10:6). Those who hunger and thirst for righteousness will not escape the blessings of God.

As God leads us in paths of righteousness for His name's sake (Ps. 23:3), what specific blessings can His righteous disciples look forward to receiving? Consider 11 inspiring examples from Proverbs.

First, God will give the righteous treasures without trouble. "In the house of the righteous there is much treasure, but trouble befalls the income of the wicked" (Pro. 15:6). This is not a guarantee that you will be rich, but it is a promise that your income, whether great or small, will not be plagued by trouble. The wicked have no assurance that their paychecks will not be accompanied by trouble.

Second, the righteous will experience answered prayers and closeness with God. "The LORD is far from the wicked, but he hears the prayer of the righteous" (15:29). Taking into account the Hebrew parallelism in this verse, we see that God answers the prayers of the righteous because He is especially close to them. It is the nearness of God that results in answered prayer, and the nearness of God was a reward of being righteous. Therefore, as James 5:16 says, "The prayer of a righteous person has great power."

Third, the righteous are endowed with boldness or fearlessness. "The wicked flee when no one pursues, but the righteous are bold as a lion" (Pro. 28:1). The simple fact is that much fear, anxiety, and paranoia, which cause people to live by constantly looking in the rearview mirror, are often the result of sin, while boldness is the reward of the righteous. We could also state it this way: Righteousness results in stability. "The righteous will never be removed, but the wicked will not dwell in the land" (10:30).

Fourth, the righteous speak words of wisdom. They know what to say at the appropriate time. "The mouth of the righteous brings forth wisdom, but the perverse tongue will be cut off. The lips of the righteous know what is acceptable, but the mouth of the wicked, what is perverse" (10:31-32). This is just a positive application of Jesus' words, "'For out of the abundance of the heart the mouth speaks'" (Matt. 12:34).

Fifth, the righteous have the ability to bounce back from calamity. "Lie not in wait as a wicked man against the dwelling of the righteous; do no violence to his home; for the righteous falls seven times and rises again, but the wicked stumble in times of calamity" (Pro. 24:15-16). In the vernacular of the present day, "You can't keep a good man down."

Sixth, the righteous are blessed with increasing wisdom. "Give instruction to a wise man, and he will be still wiser; teach a righteous man, and he will increase in learning" (9:9). Righteousness leads to wisdom, and wickedness leads to stupidity. I'm not kidding. Romans 1:21-22 makes it clear that a failure to glorify God and thank Him has an adverse effect upon one's thinking: "For although they knew God, they did not honor him as God or give thanks to him, but they became futile in their thinking, and their foolish hearts were darkened. Claiming to be wise, they became fools."

Seventh, the righteous are given an enduring reputation. "The memory of the righteous is a blessing, but the name of the wicked will rot" (Pro.10:7). "For the righteous will never be moved; he will be remembered forever" (Ps. 112:6).

Eighth, the righteous are filled with joy. "An evil man is ensnared in his transgression, but a righteous man sings and rejoices" (Pro. 29:6). If we follow the Hebrew parallelism again, we see that sin leads to sorrow, while holiness leads to happiness. This is why repentance is so important; it restores to us the joy of our salvation that was forfeited by our sin (Ps. 51:12).

Ninth, another reward for righteousness is satisfaction. "The righteous has enough to satisfy his appetite, but the belly of the wicked suffers want" (Pro. 13:25). In applying this verse we don't need to limit the appetite to one's hunger for food. "What the wicked dreads will come upon him, but the desire of the righteous will be granted" (10:24). This explains why the righteous are satisfied: God has given them the desire of their heart.

Tenth, "The righteous is delivered from trouble, and the wicked walks into it instead" (11:8). This promise also extends to future generations: "Be assured, an evil person will not go unpunished, but the offspring of the righteous will be delivered" (11:21).

Finally, the righteous find peace at death. "The wicked is overthrown through his evildoing, but the righteous finds refuge in his death" (14:32). Even when the righteous are on their deathbed God's blessing is still upon them.

Manifestly, God rewarding or showing favor to the righteous is a prominent motif in the book of Proverbs. Parents should meditate upon this theme for the edification of their own souls. As a personal note: I have frequently preached this message to myself to persevere in righteousness. It's a powerful lesson that simply living a righteous life pulls down manifold blessings from God, while unrighteousness and sin brings a forfeiture of those blessings and replaces them with curses. This teaching must also be impressed upon the hearts and minds of our children, so that this worldview becomes second nature in their thinking.

11

Gossip

The Sin that Has Slain Its Tens of Thousands

Our words can bring about life or death, they can heal or wound, they can forgive or condemn, they can build up or tear down. Proverbs 14:1 says, "The wisest of women builds her house, but folly with her own hands tears it down." I've never actually seen a woman tear down her house with her hands, but I have seen more than one woman tear it down with her tongue. Men also have the capacity to wield their tongue like a wrecking ball.

One of the most damaging sins in the church today is gossip. Jim Cymbala, pastor of The Brooklyn Tabernacle, noted that while drugs, alcohol, and adultery have slain their thousands, gossip and backbiting have slain their tens of thousands. Every experienced pastor unfortunately understands the truth behind that statement. Gossip, which is spreading bad information about someone that is only destructive, is deadly.

We need discernment here, because what we sometimes call gossip isn't gossip, and what we sometimes don't consider gossip is gossip. On one occasion a member of our church was considering recommending another member for a job. He asked me if I thought this person was a good worker. I didn't, and I told him so. Did I gossip? I don't believe so. I told the truth in an appropriate context that served a constructive purpose. If, on the other hand, I had just freely and indiscriminately talked about the laziness of this person, for no particular reason than "I feel like it," that would be gossip.

"A gossip betrays a confidence, but a trustworthy man keeps a secret" (11:13, NIV). Once again, this calls for discernment. Some secrets should not be kept confidential, because keeping some secrets allows a person to continue in sinful, illegal, or dangerous behavior. If, however, you must reveal the secret to a parent or authority for the sake of the person's well-being, leave it there. Don't then also go and tell 10 of your closest friends about the situation. Keep the juicy morsel to yourself.

Gossip ruins friendships. "A dishonest man spreads strife, and a whisperer (gossip) separates close friends" (16:28). "Whoever covers an offense seeks love, but he who repeats a matter separates close friends" (17:9). Therefore, do not associate with such people (20:19).

Closely related to gossip is tattling. "He that goeth about as a talebearer revealeth secrets: therefore meddle not with him that flattereth with his lips" (20:19, KJV). This is a hard one for parents, because they like to be told when their children are misbehaving. But if you're not careful, one of your children can turn into a spy. So when is it OK, and when is it not OK, to tattle? It's OK when children are concerned about their sibling's or friend's well-being; it's not OK when children are just trying to get this sibling or friend in trouble. It's fine if cute, little Jane comes running in the house exclaiming, "Daddy, Johnny's climbing on the ladder! I'm afraid he's going to get hurt." That's very different from, "Daddy, you told Johnny not to climb on the ladder, but he deliberately disobeyed you. I think he needs a spanking, don't you?" Dad should respond, "Yes, he does...and so do you, young lady." We are warned, and must teach our children, "Do not rejoice when your enemy falls, and let not your heart be glad when he stumbles" (24:17).

The Puritan Thomas Watson said, "It makes little difference whether you carry the devil around in your mouth or your ear." It takes two to tango, and it takes two to gossip. We are involved in gossip when we spread it, and when we listen to it. If people feel comfortable telling you "the latest," why do they? If you say nothing, they will assume you agree with them. And don't be surprised if *that* gets spread around too. If you think you are being told information that you should not be privy to, you have an obligation to say so. If you hold people accountable for what they say, by perhaps suggesting that you go together to tell the appropriate person, you will find people less inclined to tell you gossip next time, or perhaps to tell anybody else for that matter.

Late one evening a pastor was seen staggering out of a bar by one of the ladies in his congregation. She was appalled, and told two others in the church, who in turn each told two others...and so the story spread like wildfire, until the whole town knew. The pastor confronted this lady in his church and explained how another gentleman in their church was struggling with alcohol, and had called him from the bar because he was in no condition to drive. The pastor was stumbling, because he was helping this man out of the bar. The lady felt terrible, but the damage had been done, and it could not be reversed. If only gossipers would learn to bite their tongue. If only Christians were bold enough to confront gossipers and make them turn around and talk to the right people. *If only*...the church could begin to be the family it's supposed to be.

12

THE BATTLE WITH BOASTING

"Let Another Praise You, and Not Your Own Mouth"

The following are issues related to the tongue that the book of Proverbs addresses: Slander, gossip, boasting, lying, flattery, dissension, quarreling, hurtful joking, tattling, and venting. It also talks about words that are wise, foolish, gracious, crooked, deceptive, gentle, harsh, as well as words that contain or conceal hatred and violence, words that are a fountain of life, words that pierce like a sword, and words that bring healing. And, believe it or not, there are others. The sheer volume of verses that mention our speech clearly indicates that this is a serious facet of the Christian life.

Here we want to address boasting or bragging. When I was a young kid, few celebrities were more inclined to strut their stuff than the heavyweight boxing champion of the world Muhammad Ali. In my head, I can still hear him saying with his distinct accent, "I am the greatest." Such boasting is nauseating. Proverbs 27:2 says, "Let another praise you, and not your own mouth; a stranger, and not your own lips." We live in a culture that says, "Sell yourself…promote yourself…praise yourself." As Christians we should feel very uncomfortable talking about how talented and gifted we are, even if it may be necessary at times, such as at a job interview.

Why are we such an arrogant, boasting people? We may be a little more subtle than Muhammad Ali, yet we know how to drop hints to let others know how great we are. We tell stories where we're the hero...the hard worker...the smart one. We talk about the good deal we got on our new car. Why don't we ever talk about how foolish we were to spend so much money for our new car? When was the last time you heard somebody admit that he or she got ripped off or taken advantage of? It's been a while, hasn't it? Why? You know why—because that could make a person look bad. Isn't one of our greatest fears, the fear that others will not think too highly of us? Interestingly, the apostle Paul had the exact opposite concern. He said, "Even if I should choose to boast, I would not be a fool, because I would be speaking the truth. But I refrain, so no one will think more of me than is warranted by what I do or say" (2 Cor. 12:6, NIV). You know your battle with boasting is under control when you fear that others may think more highly of you than is appropriate.

Assuming that maybe—just maybe—you have a little boasting to deal with in your life, how can you (and I) overcome this sin that is so repulsive to others, as well as to God? Consider three suggestions.

For starters, it helps to recognize that absolutely everything that we have, do, and are is because of God's grace and goodness. "What do you have that you did not receive? If then you received it, why do you boast as if you did not receive it?" (1 Cor. 4:7). This verse is one verse among thousands that supports my Calvinism. I'm a Calvinist, because the Bible teaches that all we have comes from the hand of a sovereign God, including our repentance and faith in Christ. Yes, we are commanded to repent and believe, but Scripture is equally clear that it is God who grants repentance (2 Tim. 2:24-26; Acts 5:31) and faith (Phil. 1:29, Eph. 2:8-9). If you were personally responsible for the origin of your repentance and faith, then we could expect the church to gather around you, pat you on the back, and sing praises to your name for being so intelligent, while so many other dummies in the world aren't bright enough to repent and believe in Christ. Of course we all know this is absurd, but why? Because it is God who grants repentance and faith, and thus deserves *all* the glory.

Second, boast in your weaknesses. Paul said, "If I must boast, I will boast of the things that show my weakness" (2 Cor. 11:30). It's another paradox of the Christian life that our weaknesses result in strength. "Therefore I will boast all the more gladly of my weaknesses, so that the power of Christ may rest upon me… For when I am weak, then I am strong" (2 Cor. 12:9-10). Ironically, some Christians are anemic and ineffective in ministry, because they're so strong.

Finally, boast in the Lord, and in what He has done. The apostle Paul provides us with a great example: "But far be it from me to boast except in the cross of our Lord Jesus Christ, by which the world has been crucified to me, and I to the world" (Gal. 6:14). God has made Christ "our wisdom and our righteousness and sanctification and redemption. Therefore, as it is written, 'Let the one who boasts, boast in the Lord.'" (1 Cor. 1:30-31).

Many years ago I was talking with a co-worker who was partying too much. I told her that I used to live like that, until I turned to Christ. She said, "You just grew up and got your act together." I confessed that I tried to get my act together, but I couldn't do it, until I cried out to God for help. Even though that interaction took place many years ago, I can still recall that in the midst of it God firmly impressed upon me: "Don't you dare take credit for what I did in your life!" It's impossible to boast in our achievements and victories, and boast in the Lord, simultaneously. Christian boasting is always and only in the Lord.

13

Quit Quarreling

Often We Need to Just Move Along and Dig Another Well

My thesis for this chapter is very simple, but it will be difficult to apply: It is never right to quarrel, so quit quarreling. I intentionally used the word *never* to stress the absoluteness of the command. Our relativistic age wants to think that there are exceptions to every command. And of course we tend to imagine that *our* situation is the exception to the rule. However, there are no exceptions. God's word is not a wax nose that bends to fit our seemingly unique experience. Furthermore, God did not fail to take our circumstances into account when He gave His commands. The Bible is clear: "The beginning of strife is like letting out water, so quit before the quarrel breaks out" (Pro. 17:14).

Regrettably, all of us know the heartache of quarreling. Therefore, to put an end to this sin it may be helpful to examine a few reasons for why quarreling happens. First, quarreling sometimes results from hubris. Whether we mean to say this or not, an arrogant spirit communicates, "You're an idiot. You don't have the intellectual prowess or spiritual discernment I have. You'd be a fool not to follow my insight." Such an attitude is a surefire way to provoke a quarrel.

Second, quarreling is often the result of rebellion. Our egalitarian, antiestablishment, revolutionary culture despises what God has instituted, namely authority structures. Unless sin is involved there is to be unilateral submission by citizens to the government, by employees to employers, by a wife to her husband, by children to their parents, by a congregation to its elders. Many quarrels are simply a defiance of God-given authority—and they are completely unnecessary.

Third, we quarrel because we're selfish. James pinpoints the origin of murder, fights, and quarrels: "You desire and do not have, so you murder. You covet and cannot obtain, so you fight and quarrel" (Jam. 4:2). Sometimes we adults can be just as childish as the 2-year-old boy who refuses to share his Tonka truck with his friend.

Fourth, quarrels break out when the flesh takes over. The works of the flesh are evident, and among them are many quarrel-inducing characteristics, including enmity, strife, jealousy, fits of anger, rivalries, dissensions, divisions, envy, and things like these (Gal. 5:19-20).

Finally, we quarrel because we're convinced we can change situations and people through quarreling. But quarreling is never God's appointed means for change. Paul instructed Timothy, "And the Lord's servant must not be quarrelsome but kind to everyone, able to teach, patiently enduring evil, correcting his opponents with gentleness. God may perhaps grant them repentance leading to a knowledge of the truth, and they may come to their senses and escape from the snare of the devil, after being captured by him to do his will" (2 Tim. 2:24-26). God's appointed means for change is not quarreling, but kindness, patience, and gentleness (the fruit of the Spirit versus the works of the flesh). If we apply these means, "God may perhaps grant them repentance." It is God who changes people—period. If we get to be a part of His work—great, but if we don't apply His means, we will only get in His way and hinder the process.

There are many different ways we could apply this last point. For example, when it comes to evangelism, we need to be careful that apologetics isn't just intellectual quarreling. The assumption seems to be that if you can win the argument, you can win the soul. But as one of my college professors warned me, based on his own experience, if our attitude is not kind, patient, and gentle, we can win the argument but lose the soul.

You might be *right*, Mr. Employee, about what is best for the company, but it is *wrong* to quarrel with those above you. You might be right, Mrs. Wife, but if you quarrel with your husband, don't be surprised if he starts spending more time in the workshop (Pro. 21:9).

"It is an honor for a man to keep aloof from strife, but every fool will be quarreling" (Pro. 20:3).

"But what if I'm wronged?" you ask.

Here's the hard answer: "Allow yourself to be wronged."

"Yeah, but," you protest, "that could cost me."

Perhaps it could. But I still insist that we need to *trust God*...as Isaac did. This is a faith matter. We read in Genesis: "But when Isaac's servants dug in the valley and found there a well of spring water, the herdsmen of Gerar quarreled with Isaac's herdsmen saying, 'The water is ours'" (Gen. 26:19-20). How does Isaac respond? He simply moves on and digs another well. Unfortunately, a quarrel broke out over that well, too. Once again, he avoids the contention and moves on and digs yet another well. This time they did not quarrel over it, and Isaac concludes, '"For now the Lord has made room for us, and we shall be fruitful in the land'" (vs. 22). Be honorable, be wise, keep aloof from strife, and God will bless you also.

14

A Lying Tongue

A Meditation on Abominable Lying and Acceptable Lying

"There are six things that the LORD hates, seven that are an abomination to him: haughty eyes, *a lying tongue*, and hands that shed innocent blood, a heart that devises wicked plans, feet that make haste to run to evil, *a false witness who breathes out lies*, and one who sows discord among brothers" (Pro. 6:16-19, emphasis added). These verses underscore God's hatred of lying. In a list of seven things that are an abomination to God, lying makes the list twice.

"A lying tongue hates its victims, and a flattering mouth works ruin" (26:28). Lying is a predatory act of hatred that takes advantage of people. As if this wasn't bad enough, Proverbs describes lying even more violently: "A man who bears false witness against his neighbor is like a war club, or a sword, or a sharp arrow" (25:18). Lying is not only an act of hatred; it is also an act of war. Solomon compares a liar to the weapons used in warfare to kill the enemy. I highlight this violent, war aspect for two reasons. First, this aspect shows the seriousness of lying. The irony is that we sometimes lie to keep the peace (so we think), when it is actually a declaration of war. Second, this violent, war aspect shows the context in which lying is permissible.

The sixth commandment says, "Thou shalt not murder." Thoughtful Christians know that this command doesn't forbid killing in a just war or applying the death penalty to murderers, where God commands the government to take the life of the guilty. This isn't a contradiction. In certain contexts, like war, there are exceptions. The ninth commandment against lying should be interpreted in a similar way.

Here's a question that is frequently raised in Christian ethics classes: "During WWII, if the Nazis asked if you were hiding Jews in your home, when you were, should you tell them the truth?" One of Corrie ten Boom's relatives thought that they were required by God to always, without exception, tell the truth. So when the ten Booms' house was raided she admitted that they were hiding Jews under the table. When the soldiers started to look, she laughed as if she were playing with them, because, in fact, Jews were hiding under the floor that was under the table. Technically she told the truth, but at the same time her laughter was a way of deceiving—of lying. Let's not play these games. When we give others a false impression we are lying. Lying also includes such euphemisms as white lies, exaggerations, stretching the truth, spinning the truth, slanting the truth, presenting only one side of the truth, or telling a half-truth, which is a full lie. But the question still stands: In the context of war, are we required by God to tell the truth, the whole truth, and nothing but the truth?

A few biblical examples make the answer clear. First, the Hebrew midwives were told by the king of Egypt to kill all the Israelite sons they delivered. "But the midwives feared God and did not do as the king of Egypt commanded them, but let the male children live" (Ex. 1:17). So the king confronted them, and asked why they let the boys live. "The midwives said to Pharaoh, 'Because the Hebrew women are not like the Egyptian women, for they are vigorous and give birth before the midwife comes to them'" (vs. 19). Simply put, the midwives were big, fat liars—*because they feared God.* "So God dealt well with the midwives... And because the midwives feared God, he gave them families" (vv. 20-21). God basically says, "Well done, good and faithful servants," and He rewards them for their God-fearing lying by blessing them with children of their own.

Next, look at James' use of Rahab as an example. In the context, James is showing "that faith apart from works is useless" (Jam. 2:20). James argues that true faith is always accompanied by works. He uses Abraham and his willingness to sacrifice Isaac as an example, and then he uses Rahab as another example. But what makes Rahab so interesting is the "work" that James mentions. He writes, "And in the same way was not also Rahab the prostitute justified by works when she received the messengers and sent them out by another way?" (vs. 25). Rahab's faith-validating work was that of *lying*. Her faith was demonstrated when she sent the spies "out by another way"—a way that was different from the way indicated in the lie she told the officials. You may not have thought this way before, but some lying flows from faith and pleases God.

Finally, after King Saul is rejected by the Lord from being king over Israel, the prophet Samuel is told to go and anoint a new king from among the sons of Jesse the Bethlehemite. Samuel responds, "'How can I go? If Saul hears it, he will kill me.' And the LORD said, 'Take a heifer with you and say, 'I have come to sacrifice to the LORD' ' " (1 Sam. 16:2). So, Samuel lies to King Saul *as he was instructed by God.* Case closed.

However, remember that an allowable context for lying is war. If you lie to someone you're implicitly saying, "I hate you, and we're at war with each other." If you're not at war, or you don't want to be at war, then don't lie. The foundation of all healthy relationships is trust, and such relationships cannot survive for very long without it. So if you want to enjoy good relationships, avoid lying (of all stripes) like the plague.

15

Sovereignty, Not Chance

This Even Applies to the Dice Rolled in Las Vegas

To say that God is sovereign, is to say that He is the Lord and King in His universe, and that He "works out everything in conformity with the purpose of His will" (Eph. 1:11 NIV). God orders and directs every event, in order to fulfill His purposes, and to bring glory and honor to His name. And nothing—absolutely nothing—is outside of or beyond His sovereign control.

The Heidelberg Catechism addresses the sovereignty of God in answer 27: "The Almighty and everywhere present power of God upholds heaven and earth with all creatures, and so governs them that herbs and grass [don't overlook the minute details that God controls], rain and drought, fruitful and barren years, meat and drink, health and sickness, riches and poverty, yea, all things, come not by chance, but by His Fatherly hand."

I know this is not an easy doctrine to fully embrace at first. It may take struggling and wrestling before we are ready to praise God for His sovereignty. Jonathan Edwards testified about his own struggle with this difficult doctrine: "From my childhood up, my mind had been full of objections against the doctrine of God's sovereignty... It used to appear like a horrible doctrine to me... [But] there has been a wonderful alteration in my mind, in respect to the doctrine of God's sovereignty... I have often since had not only a conviction, but a delightful conviction. The doctrine has very often appeared exceeding pleasant, bright, and sweet. Absolute sovereignty is what I love to ascribe to God. But my first conviction was not so."

Jesus took great delight in God's sovereignty. We read in Luke 10:21-22: "In that same hour he rejoiced in the Holy Spirit and said, 'I thank you, Father, Lord of heaven and earth, that you have hidden these things from the wise and understanding and revealed them to little children; yes, Father, for such was your gracious will. All things have been handed over to me by my Father, and no one knows who the Son is except the Father, or who the Father is except the Son and anyone to whom the Son chooses to reveal him.'" This is one of only two passages in the Gospels where we're told that Jesus is glad or rejoices. The other is John 11:14-15, where Jesus says, "'Lazarus has died, and for your sake I am glad that I was not there, so that you may believe.'" Putting the two passages together, it seems that nothing brings Jesus greater joy than the sovereign work of His Father that results in faith.

Why do we fail to understand such a basic doctrine? I submit to you that too often our thinking is more American than biblical, and more atheistic than Christian. What do we often say when we narrowly miss getting into a terrible car accident by a few inches? "Wow, was I lucky!" Or, we attend a sports event with tens of thousands of people, and we run into a friend we haven't seen for years, and think, "What a coincidence. What are the chances of that happening?" Such talk is completely foreign to the writers of sacred Scripture. Luck, coincidence, and chance have no place in a universe governed and controlled by an omniscient, omnipotent, omnipresent sovereign Lord.

Proverbs 16:33 says, "The lot is cast into the lap, but its every decision is from the LORD." Today we would say that God even controls the outcome of the dice that are rolled in Las Vegas. I love this verse, because it shows that nothing is too small or insignificant for God to control. This is important, especially when we realize that "small" things can have huge consequences. Some of you are familiar with the poem: "For want of a nail the shoe was lost; for want of a shoe the horse was lost; for want of a horse the rider was lost; for want of a rider the battle was lost; for want of a battle the kingdom was lost." World history can be altered because of one little seemingly insignificant nail.

R.C. Sproul said one of his childhood heroes, racecar driver Bill Vukovich, was killed in the 1955 Indianapolis 500 when he was going around a turn and his car lost control because a 10-cent cotter pin broke. Sproul's account may be apocryphal, yet, nevertheless, the record does indicate that Bill Vukovich's death at Indy began with a "small" event. Vukovich became ensnared in a chain reaction accident that started when Rodger Ward's car spun out—due, a report says, to a *gust of wind*. Regardless, the point is the same.

In the Battle of Fort Duquesne during the French and Indian War, a young lieutenant colonel had two horses shot out from underneath him. At one point in the battle a bullet from an enemy rifle went through one side of his shirt and out the other as it was flapping behind him in the wind, missing his body by mere inches. That young lieutenant colonel survived that battle and became the first President of the United States of America. Was George Washington *lucky?* Or was a sovereign God controlling the flying bullets? If God is not in control of everything, including nails, the wind, and flying bullets, our lives and this world are spinning out of control, and we are at the mercy of whimsical chance. If He is in control—and He is—then we can confidently rejoice always.

Don't Live Like an Atheist

Explanations of luck, coincidence, or chance are how atheists view the "random" happenings of life in a closed universe without God. When we use their rhetoric, we downplay at best, or deny at worst, the loving, personal involvement of God in our daily lives. Is it any wonder that we don't immediately thank God for the blessings that come our way, or petition Him in prayer the moment tragedy strikes, or ask for strength to resist temptation when we see it headed our way? If we go through our day with little or no thought of God and His involvement in our lives, we are "practical atheists."

The inspired writers did not think in terms of luck, coincidence, or chance. Even "natural" events are clearly ascribed to God. Yes, God has set the water cycles in motion, as well as the constellations in their seasons, but the writers prefer to say that God causes His sun to rise, and that He sends the rain (Matt. 5:45), as well as the lightning and the wind (Ps. 135:7). In the Bible, women don't just "get pregnant," rather we read that the Lord opens the womb (Gen. 29:31, 33; 30:1-2, 17, 19, 22). And, it is your heavenly Father who feeds the birds of the air and clothes the grass of the field (Matt. 6:26, 30).

James admonishes those with a propensity to marginalize God's involvement in their schedule: "Now listen, you who say, 'Today or tomorrow we will go to this or that city, spend a year there, carry on business and make money…' Instead, you ought to say, '*If it is the Lord's will*, we will live and do this or that.' As it is, you boast and brag. All such boasting is evil" (James 4:13, 15-16 NIV, emphasis added). The point here is simple, yet profound: Don't go through life acting as if God isn't sovereignly in control or has no say in your daily decisions—again, this is how atheists live.

Since everything that happens to us is under God's sovereign control, then all of life should be lived in response to Him. If troubles are from Him, then we petition Him. If blessings are from Him, then we thank Him (James 5:13-14). The sovereignty of God should cause us to live every single day with an acute awareness of His loving and personal involvement in every aspect of our lives. In a world of apparent chaos, it is comforting to know that what happens to us is not left to dumb luck, coincidence, or chance, but to God's sovereign will.

In fact, I know of no other doctrine that will provide believers with such a sure and solid foundation in the worst of times, including the death of a loved one, than the sovereignty of God. George Mueller found solace in this doctrine when his wife was dying. He prayed after he discovered that his wife had rheumatic fever: "Yes, my Father, the times of my darling wife are in Thy hands. Thou wilt do the very best thing for her, and for me, whether life or death. If it may be, raise up yet again my precious wife—Thou are able to do it, though she is so ill; but howsoever Thou dealest with me, only help me to continue to be perfectly satisfied with Thy holy will."

It was not God's will to raise her up again, but Mueller trusted in God's sovereignty. He said, "I bow, I am satisfied with the will of my Heavenly Father, I seek by perfect submission to his holy will to glorify him, I kiss continually the hand that has afflicted me… Without an effort my inmost soul habitually joys in the joy of that loved departed one. Her happiness gives joy to me. My dear daughter and I would not have her back, were it possible to produce it by the turn of a hand. God himself has done it; we are satisfied with him."[19] Since God is sovereign, all that happens to us *is* His will. As a result, we can be certain that He has a good and wise purpose in all that comes our way (Rom. 8:28).

If there is one maverick molecule outside of God's sovereign control, then God's purposes can be thwarted and "chance" rules the universe. But as Job testified confidently, "I know that you can do all things, and that no purpose of yours can be thwarted" (Job 42:2). This should fill us with calm assurance. If God has a plan for my life—and He certainly does—then nobody and nothing can stop or sidetrack that plan. From the womb to the tomb, nothing happens by chance, but by sovereign decree. When we were in our mother's womb God formed our inward parts and knitted us together as He saw fit for His purposes. And before we were even born and saw the light of day, God had already ordained the days of our lives (Ps. 139:13-16), as well as the time and place where we would live (Acts 17:26). Therefore, from one perspective, we are invincible and immortal until God's work for us is done. Let's live like it. God is on His sovereign throne, and He never ceases for a moment from working out everything in conformity with the purpose of His will (Eph. 1:11).

Harmonizing Divine Sovereignty and Human Responsibility

One of the first questions that may come to mind when you hear about the sovereignty of God is this: "If God is ordering and directing all events to work out everything in conformity with the purpose of His will (Eph. 1:11), then how can anyone be held responsible for their actions?" At first glance, divine sovereignty and human responsibility seem as incompatible as oil and water, and appear to defy logic. Therefore, our natural inclination is to cling to sovereignty and reject responsibility, or to cling to responsibility and reject sovereignty. This inclination is the result of finite, common-sense, human reasoning, rather than submitting to the infinite wisdom of God's Word, where both truths are clearly taught to coexist in perfect harmony.

Let us recognize that we are dealing with an "antinomy" (an apparent contradiction between two otherwise reasonable principles or laws). An antinomy exists when two truths placed side by side *seem* incompatible with one another. "There are cogent reasons for believing each of them; each rests on clear and solid evidence; but it is a mystery to you how they can be squared with each other. You see that each must be true on its own, but you do not see how they can both be true together."[20]

The Bible does not claim to tell us precisely *how* divine sovereignty and human responsibility can be mutually compatible, it only insists that they are. Theologians sometimes call this duality *compatibilism*, since God's sovereignty and human responsibility are *compatible*. Without a doubt, we are dealing with mysterious and complex truths here; however, neither truth should be sacrificed for the sake of the other, nor should either truth be softened or watered down. Both are to be asserted and upheld in the most unqualified terms, as they are throughout the pages of Scripture.

The Bible is replete with compelling examples that show both truths coexisting harmoniously. The crucifixion of Christ provides an excellent illustration. Jesus tells His disciples at the Last Supper, '"For the Son of Man goes as it has been determined, but woe to that man by whom he is betrayed!"' (Lk. 22:22). In other words, the cross was part of the sovereign plan of God, while, at the same time, Judas will be held accountable for betraying Jesus. On the day of Pentecost, Peter says, '"Men of Israel, hear these words: Jesus of Nazareth, a man attested to you by God with mighty works and wonders and signs that God did through him in your midst, as you yourselves know—this Jesus, delivered up according to the definite plan and foreknowledge of God, you crucified and killed by the hands of lawless men"' (Acts 2:22-23; see also 4:24-28). Notice that Peter recognizes God's sovereignty *and* man's responsibility in the death of Christ. God had a purpose in the death of His Son, and wicked men also had a purpose in the death of His Son. Again, we concede that there is a great mystery operating here, but God's sovereign purposes are interwoven with the evil purposes of men that they are responsible for. However, God's purposes ultimately prevail, for this is what it means to be sovereign. As God Himself asserted, '"I am God, and there is none like me, declaring the end from the beginning and from ancient times things not yet done, saying, "My counsel shall stand, and I will accomplish all my purpose" ' " (Isa. 46:9b-10). C.H. Spurgeon was once asked if he could reconcile divine sovereignty and human responsibility. "I wouldn't try," he replied; "I never reconcile friends."

Compatibilism is at the core of Romans 8:28, which is one of the most comforting verses in the Bible during times of tragedy: "And we know that in all things God works for the good of those who love him, who have been called according to his purpose" (NIV). Those who love God, and are called by God, can rest assured that He is working for their good "in all things." Not *in spite of* all things, or *after* all things, but *in* all things. As with the crucifixion of Christ, God is at work in the evil events and tragedies of our life, in order to bring about His good will for us. This is almost unfathomable. It takes a firm faith in God's Word to believe this.

Throughout Joseph's life, in the Old Testament, we find the phrases: "the LORD was with Joseph" and "the LORD was with him" (Gen. 39:2, 3, 21, 23). These simple phrases are meant to remind us that while it appears that men's intentions are gaining the upper hand, God is right there with Joseph. And He is right there with us—even if it seems that He has abandoned us—and His prevailing intentions are at work. In our finite minds it's nearly impossible to comprehend two interwoven intentions operating simultaneously, but this is what the Bible teaches (Gen. 50:20) and what we must believe. Faith is required to see beyond the external circumstances of life into the mysterious ways of God where He remains sovereign and we remain responsible.

16

"Go to the Ant, O Sluggard"

Laziness: The Sin by Which We Ignore Our Obligations

Once upon a time in a faraway land, there was a small village in which lived four men, named Everybody, Somebody, Anybody, and Nobody. Now in this village there was a significant task that had to be done, and Everybody was asked to do it. Everybody neglected to do it, because he was sure that Somebody would do it. Anybody could have done it, but Nobody did it. Somebody got upset about this, since it was Everybody's job. However, Everybody thought that Anybody could have done it, yet Nobody was aware that Everybody wouldn't do it. In the end, Everybody blamed Somebody, while Nobody did the job that Anybody could have done in the first place.

What's the moral of the story? The next time there is an important job that everybody is asked to do, somebody needs to take responsibility and forget about the fact that anybody can do it, because if somebody doesn't do it, nobody will do it again, and the whole village will suffer. Whether the village represents a neighborhood or a church or a family, the truth remains the same—laziness hurts all involved.

What is laziness? It's not an occasional nap. It's the sin by which we ignore our obligations. Laziness is the sin of omission, rather than commission. And it could be that on the Day of Judgment our sins of omission will outnumber our sins of commission. For example, Jesus talked about judgment, and of when He will say to those on His left, "'Depart from me, you cursed, into the eternal fire prepared for the devil and his angels. For I was hungry and you gave me no food, I was thirsty and you gave me no drink...'" (Matt. 25:41-42). They are judged for laziness, sins of omission, neglecting their obligations.

Laziness is a destructive sin, causing a lot more damage than we often think. How many marriages end in divorce, not because of adultery or abuse, but simple laziness? Donald Trump's second wife told her husband, "We need to work at our marriage." He responded, "I work at my work, I don't want to work at my marriage." And it's public knowledge how that marriage ended.

Laziness is a serious sin, but it's not a complicated sin. We can learn from an ant: "Go to the ant, O sluggard; consider her ways, and be wise. Without having any chief, officer, or ruler, she prepares her bread in summer and gathers her food in harvest" (Pro. 6:6-8). Also, laziness is another one of those deceptive sins. The whole world can see that a certain man lacks initiative, except the lazy man himself. He is blind to his own sin, which is why he needs the mirror of God's Word. To help us recognize laziness in ourselves or others, let's consider four characteristics of a sluggard.

First, lazy people are full of excuses. "The sluggard says, 'There is a lion outside! I shall be killed in the streets!'" (Pro. 22:13). You might have expected this verse to read, "The *coward* says..." However, this verse isn't addressing fear, but laziness. This sluggard is making up excuses for why he can't go outside and get his work done. Douglas Wilson quips that this is the ancient equivalent of "The dog ate my homework," or "Aliens kidnapped me—what year is it?"[21] This bum is trying to justify his laziness, but nobody is buying his lame excuses. The sympathy he seeks will not come, since the lion is a figment of his lazy imagination.

Next, lazy people are a source of irritation to those who send them on an errand. "Like vinegar to the teeth and smoke to the eyes, so is the sluggard to those who send him" (Pro. 10:26). I wonder how many children needlessly irritate their parents by not doing what they're told to do. This may seem like a little thing, but if you can't follow orders at home today, you won't follow them at work tomorrow. When you're younger you irritate your parents, when you're older you irritate your boss, and don't be surprised if he or she fires you.

This leads to the third characteristic—lazy people struggle financially. "How long will you lie there, O sluggard? When will you arise from your sleep? A little sleep, a little slumber, a little folding of the hands to rest, and poverty will come upon you like a robber, and want like an armed man" (Pro. 6:9-11). Many things cause people to struggle financially, such as having champagne tastes on a beer budget, but laziness is almost a sure guarantee that you'll end up in the poorhouse. The metaphor of poverty in the form of a robber coming on the unsuspecting lazy man is a good one, because this is how the sluggard feels. He doesn't know quite what hit him, but he's now in a poverty quagmire. Perhaps he thinks he's unlucky. I don't believe in luck, but if I did, it would work this way: Work hard and you'll be lucky; ignore the alarm clock, roll over on your bed like a door on its hinges, and you'll be unlucky—a lot.

The fourth characteristic of the sluggard may seem like a contradiction at first, but it isn't: Lazy people are busy—sometimes extremely busy—doing things they shouldn't be doing. This is worth pointing out, because some people who appear to be hardworking on the surface, and to outsiders, are actually quite slothful. The problem is that in the frenzy of all their activities and busyness they're neglecting those responsibilities they ought to be taking care of first.

"Prepare your work outside; get everything ready for yourself in the field, and after that build your house" (Pro. 24:27). This verse reminds us of the need to get our priorities straight. First we plow the field and plant the crops, and then we can put up those new drapes in the living room. Lazy people love to do what is easier or more fun, and it may keep them occupied for hours on end, but in the meantime their obligations to their family or job or school are being disregarded. Allow me to move from teaching to meddling, with a couple of present day applications. Ladies, it might be more fun (and appear to be more spiritual) to be involved in that ministry group or women's group, but your first priority is taking care of the mundane but God-glorifying housework. Could it be that your participation in other activities and interests is a sign of laziness?

Men, it's great that you're willing to work overtime and be involved with the school board or some worthy political cause, but perhaps, despite what others may think, you're really lazy. It's a lot easier and more enjoyable to participate in these different endeavors, but your wife and kids may need you at home a little more; God forbid that we should be too busy to spend time with those we love the most.

Parents, if you allow your children to drift into laziness—and by the way they never *drift* into discipline, they have to be taught that—you are, according to Proverbs, preparing them for a life of poverty, where they have to beg to get by (20:4). Also, their life will be one of frustration (13:4); life will be hard, and it will seem to them that there is always some obstacle in their way, while everybody else is on the smooth road (15:19); their lot will be forced labor (12:24);

and all this will bring shame upon the parents (10:5). So how can we help our children not drift into laziness? Consider three points.

First, teach responsibility—and teach this by letting your children suffer the consequences of laziness and irresponsibility. Don't subsidize laziness. One of the best things we can do for those who are able but unwilling to work (I'm not addressing those who are unable but willing to work) is—get ready for my recommendation for a new government program—absolutely NOTHING. Let them fall, and let them feel the full impact of their laziness. Sometimes we're more compassionate than God, who said, "If anyone is not willing to work, let him not eat" (2 Thess. 3:10). However, let me interject one caveat. If we have to choose between grace and the letter of the law, let's err on the side of grace.

Second, reward hard work. This is the flip side of the first point. Paul wrote, "For it is written in the Law of Moses, 'You shall not muzzle an ox when it treads out the grain.' Is it for oxen that God is concerned? Does he not speak entirely for our sake? It was written for our sake, because the plowman should plow in hope and the thresher thresh in hope of sharing in the crop" (1 Cor. 9:9-10). Parents have asked if it's appropriate to give their kids an allowance for doing chores at home. I think it is. They shouldn't expect to be paid for everything they do, but on the other hand why should they have to wait until they're 18 or older to learn that hard work pays. Proverbs is clear that diligent labor usually is rewarded financially, so why not teach that to our children verbally, as well as with quarters or crisp dollar bills.

Third, if our children are to avoid laziness they must avoid lazy people, who will inevitably rub off on them. Paul gave this instruction that many think is harsh: "Now we command you, brothers, in the name of our Lord Jesus Christ, that you keep away from any brother who is walking in idleness" (2 Thess. 3:6). Paul went on to say, "For we hear that some among you walk in idleness, not busy at work, but busybodies" (vs. 11). If you're not busy with God-glorifying work, you're sinning more than you need to; laziness leads to other sins, it's that simple. What set the stage for David's sin with Bathsheba was laziness. He neglected his royal responsibility to led the armies of Israel: "In the spring of the year, the time when kings go out to battle, David sent Joab… David remained at Jerusalem" (2 Sam. 11:1). If David had been out on the battlefield leading his men, he never would have had time for Bathsheba. If work doesn't fill your schedule, something else will fill the void—and too often it doesn't honor God.

17

WARNINGS ABOUT WEALTH

Putting Wealth in Perspective, Before We Consider How to Acquire It

True conversion will always be reflected in one's use of money. Martin Luther said, "There are three conversions necessary: the conversion of the heart, the mind, and the purse." And of these three, it may well be that the conversion of the purse is the most difficult. The truth is that we are all very closely associated with our money, so that what we do with our money says a great deal about us, and about our spiritual condition. And we can be sure that if the lordship of Jesus Christ hasn't penetrated our wallets, it hasn't penetrated our souls either.

John the Baptist understood the connection between true repentance and how a person handled his money and possessions. He exhorted the people, '"Bear fruits in keeping with repentance;"' (Lk. 3:8). In other words, fruits that show their repentance is real and not just empty rhetoric; fruits that relate to one's money and possessions.

John addressed three groups of people: the crowds, tax collectors, and soldiers. He told the crowds, '"Whoever has two tunics is to share with him who has none, and whoever has food is to do likewise'" (vs. 11). To the tax collectors he said, '"Collect no more than you are authorized to do"' (vs. 13). He commanded the soldiers, '"Do not extort money from anyone by threats or by false accusation, and be content with your wages"' (vs. 14). A positive response to John's message would validate the veracity of their repentance. We can conclude that since repentance is the *beginning* of Christianity, a relationship with God through Jesus Christ, we can also say that Christianity *begins* with a change in our perspective toward and use of money.

Money is a monumental issue, which is why the Bible has about 2,350 verses on money and possessions, more than twice that which is devoted to faith and prayer combined. Jesus said more about money than he did about heaven and hell together. And 16 of his 38 parables deal with money and possessions. This subject is obviously important, so it would behoove us to consider six warnings about wealth. However, by stating these warnings, I'm not saying that wealth is automatically or inherently bad—it isn't. In fact, after addressing "Warnings About Wealth" we will consider "How to Acquire Wealth." If God didn't want us to acquire wealth He wouldn't have provided us with so many clear principles for doing so. Yet we must always be cognizant of the limitations and dangers connected with money and prosperity. Jesus wasn't kidding when He said, after the rich, young ruler turned away from eternal life, because it meant turning away from his money god, '"How difficult it is for those who have wealth to enter the kingdom of God! For it is easier for a camel to go through the eye of a needle than for a rich person to enter the kingdom of God"' (Lk. 18:24-25). These words alone should provoke a healthy fear of money. With this being said, let's consider six additional warnings about wealth.

For starters, in our debt-ridden culture we need the reminder that debt is a form of slavery. "The rich rules over the poor, and the borrower is the slave of the lender" (Pro. 22:7). While borrowing money is not necessarily a sin, it does have many negative consequences—including headaches, as you rack your brain trying to figure out how you're going to pay off all that debt. One of the blessings of God is that of lending, instead of borrowing. God promised the Israelites if they walked in obedience, '"The LORD will open to you his good treasury, the heavens, to give the rain to your land in its season and to bless all the work of your hands. And you shall lend to many nations, but you shall not borrow"' (Deut. 28:12).

When it comes to buying things, it might help if we ask ourselves, "Can I afford it?" rather than, "Can I afford the payments?" Car salespeople employ this strategy, because it gives the impression that you can afford more than you actually can. Installments of $200 a month don't sound nearly as bad as $10,000. It's fascinating how this whole concept of making payments has changed over the years. During WWI the vast majority of homes were owned outright. If you did have a mortgage, the average length of the mortgage was less than one year. By WWII the average length of a mortgage was four to five years, and it took a special act of Congress to legalize mortgages over seven years. Today, 15-year mortgages are relatively rare; 30-year mortgages are common; 40-year mortgages are not uncommon; and in Japan there are even 90-year mortgages now, which means that parents are not only enslaving themselves, but also their children, and maybe even their grandchildren. If "the borrower is the slave of the lender," are we really free? Again, it's not necessarily a sin to have debt or to be a slave, but as Paul said of literal slavery, "If you can gain your freedom, do so."

The second warning about wealth is to realize that a sinner's wealth will be turned over to the righteous. "A good man leaves an inheritance to his children's children, but the sinner's wealth is laid up for the righteous" (Pro.

13:22). There are many examples of this in the Bible. When the Israelites left Egypt they plundered the Egyptians on the way out: "The people of Israel had also done as Moses told them, for they had asked the Egyptians for silver and gold jewelry and for clothing. And the LORD had given the people favor in the sight of the Egyptians, so that they let them have what they asked. Thus they plundered the Egyptians" (Ex. 12:35-36).

Then, 40 years later, when the Israelites finally made it to the Promised Land, they inherited immense riches that the ungodly nations had been unwittingly storing up for them. On the edge of the Promised Land, Moses told the Israelites, '"And when the LORD your God brings you into the land that he swore to your fathers, to Abraham, to Isaac, and to Jacob, to give you—with great and good cities that you did not build, and houses full of all good things that you did not fill, and cisterns that you did not dig, and vineyards and olive trees that you did not plant—and when you eat and are full, then take care lest you forget the LORD, who brought you out of the land of Egypt, out of the house of slavery"' (Deut. 6:10-12). In a world governed by a sovereign God, the righteous not only enjoy the fruit of their own labor, but they may also enjoy the fruit of their enemies' labor. Proverbs 13:22 is a warning for sinners, but a glorious promise and source of encouragement for the righteous.

Asaph confessed, "For I was envious of the arrogant when I saw the prosperity of the wicked" (Ps. 73:3). But why envy Bill Gates or Warren Buffett if all they're really doing is accumulating a massive fortune that God will—in due time—turn over to His people. Eventually, all the treasures of earth will belong to the Christians. Remember, it is the meek who will inherit the earth, and that includes its riches.

Third, eagerness for riches leads to punishment. "A faithful man will abound with blessings, but whoever hastens to be rich will not go unpunished" (Pro. 28:20). I believe this hastiness for wealth is, in part, a warning against gambling and the lottery. While the Bible doesn't explicitly condemn gambling, gambling does (often) violate many Scriptural principles. For example, gambling encourages greed, as well as materialism and discontentment with our possessions. Think of all the lottery players who dream big, because if they win they can finally purchase their dream home or a sports car or maybe a yacht. Such dreaming can be dangerous, due to the discontentment that results. This discontentment and desire for more, more, more, drives many who end up in the grip of gambling and can't break free.

Gambling can also discourage honest work. "Whoever works his land will have plenty of bread, but he who follows worthless pursuits will have plenty of poverty" (Pro. 28:19). Furthermore, gambling is a reckless investment of God-given resources. It's a statistical fact that the odds are better that you will get struck by lightning than that you will win a multimillion-dollar lottery. Besides, acquiring a huge sum of money all at once is difficult for many to handle. "An inheritance gained hastily in the beginning will not be blessed in the end" (Pro. 20:21). We all know of lottery winners or pro athletes or actors or rock stars that suddenly came into a large sum of money and it ruined them because they couldn't handle it.

Fourth, there are many things money can't buy—things that are much more valuable than money. Years ago the Beatles sang, "Money can't buy me love." Sometimes the Beatles were off base, but they got it right with that song. "Better is a dinner of herbs where love is than a fattened ox and hatred with it" (Pro. 15:17). A good reputation is better than money. "A good name is to be chosen rather than great riches, and favor is better than silver or gold" (Pro. 22:1). Integrity is to be preferred to money. "Better is a poor man who walks in his integrity than a rich man who is crooked in his ways" (Pro. 28:6). Money can't buy humility. "It is better to be of a lowly spirit with the poor than to divide the spoil with the proud" (Pro. 16:19). Peace and quiet is better than money (Pro. 17:1). A prudent wife is not for sale; she's a priceless blessing from God. "House and wealth are inherited from fathers, but a prudent wife is from the LORD" (Pro. 19:14). And, of course, I would be remiss not to point out that salvation is free, and the righteous Judge cannot be bribed. "Riches do not profit in the day of wrath, but righteousness delivers from death" (Pro. 11:4).

A fifth warning about wealth is that God can give you riches and sorrow at the same time. Understand: God can give you riches with no sorrow, or He can give you riches with sorrow, and of course the difference is whether or not the riches were acquired as a result of God's blessing. "The blessing of the LORD makes rich, and he adds no sorrow with it" (Pro. 10:22).

Even among Christians, the assumption seems to be that money automatically brings happiness, but this is not the teaching of Scripture, nor is it the testimony of many who have accumulated vast fortunes. Back in 1977, O.J. Simpson confessed, "I sit in my house in Buffalo and sometimes I `get so...lonely it's unbelievable. Life has been so good to me. I have a great wife, good kids, money, my own health—and I'm lonely and bored... I often wondered why so many rich people commit suicide. Money sure isn't a cure-all."[22]

Successful cartoonist Ralph Barton killed himself in 1931 while in a depressed state. According to one version, his suicide note read, "I have had few difficulties, many friends, great successes; I have gone from wife to wife, and from house to house, visited great countries of the world, but I am fed up with inventing devices to fill up 24 hours of the day." And you all know that much more anecdotal evidence could be provided to show that money alone doesn't bring happiness.

Referring to the Israelites grumbling and complaining in Numbers 11, Psalm 106:14-15 says as a commentary, "But they had a wanton craving in the wilderness, and put God to the test in the desert; he gave them what they asked, but sent a wasting disease among them." The King James Version translates the last verse, "And he gave them their request; but sent leanness into their soul." Also, commenting on the same episode, Psalm 78 tells how God rained down manna on the Israelites, the bread of the angels, which he sent in abundance. Then "he rained meat on them like dust… And they ate and were well filled, for he gave them what they craved. But before they had satisfied their craving, while the food was still in their mouths, the anger of God arose against them, and he killed the strongest of them and laid low the young men of Israel" (Ps. 78:27, 29-31). God may give us what we crave and ask for, but if we're not careful our requests may be accompanied by sorrow, judgment, or even death.

It's one thing to have money; it's another thing altogether to enjoy it. Solomon understood that this enjoyment wasn't to be taken for granted, since it is God-given: "Everyone also to whom God has given wealth and possessions and power to enjoy them, and to accept his lot and rejoice in his toil—this is the gift of God" (Ecc. 5:19). On the other hand, God may give a man "wealth, possessions, and honor, so that he lacks nothing of all that he desires, yet God does not give him power to enjoy them" (Ecc. 6:2).

Last, but certainly not least, is the warning that wealth can cause us to forget or deny God. Agur prayed, "(G)ive me neither poverty nor riches; feed me with the food that is needful for me, lest I be full and deny you and say, 'Who is the Lord?' or lest I be poor and steal and profane the name of my God" (Pro. 30:8-9). The poor can profane God by stealing to make ends meet, while the rich are susceptible to amnesia—"Who is the Lord?"

Moses knew about this tendency to forget God, so he addressed it even before the Israelites entered the Promised Land and inherited overflowing treasures from the nations they would conquer. To repeat the passage from Deuteronomy: '"And when the LORD your God brings you into the land that he swore to your fathers, to Abraham, to Isaac, and to Jacob, to give you—with great and good cities that you did not build, and houses full of all good things that you did not fill, and cisterns that you did not dig, and vineyards and olive trees that you did not plant—and when you eat and are full, then take care lest you forget the LORD, who brought you out of the land of Egypt, out of the house of slavery"' (Deut. 6:10-12; see also 8:11-14). When you forget God, arrogance and deception take over, which is why Moses also said, '"Beware lest you say in your heart, "My power and the might of my hand have gotten me this wealth" ' " (Deut. 8:17). Furthermore, Moses warned the people, '"And if you forget the LORD your God and go after other gods and serve them and worship them, I solemnly warn you today that you shall surely perish"' (vs. 19). Unfortunately, the Israelites did forget God and provoke His wrath (Jud. 3:7-8). Before we look down our noses at those "bumbling Israelites," let's remember that "these things happened to them as an example, but they were written down for our instruction... Therefore let anyone who thinks that he stands take heed lest he fall" (1 Cor. 10:11-12).

18

How to Acquire Wealth

Some of the Principles Will Not Be Found in Secular Books on Finances

In 1991 a national survey was published, and in it Americans were asked what they would do for $10 million. The survey revealed: 25% would abandon their family; 25% would abandon their church; 23% would become a prostitute for a week; 16% would give up their American citizenship; 16% would leave their spouse; 7% would commit murder.[23] When it comes to money, we don't want to be naïve about the impact it can exert upon our hearts.

In the Parable of the Soils, seed is sown upon four different types of soils, which represent the Word of God being sown upon four different hearts. Jesus described those having the third type heart this way: "'They are those who hear the word, but the cares of the world and the deceitfulness of riches and the desires for other things enter in and choke the word, and it proves unfruitful'" (Mk. 4:18-19). What a tragedy! No fruit, no spiritual growth, because it was strangled to death by the deceitfulness of riches and materialism. So as we talk about how to acquire wealth, which is necessary even if we're just trying to provide our families with the basic necessities of life, let's be mindful of the dangers associated with wealth.

To acquire wealth, Proverbs exhorts us to fear God and live a righteous life. Some of you might be wondering, "Fear God and live a righteous life? I need to pay the bills this week; where's the practical advice? Yes, I understand that fearing God and living righteously is essential for getting into heaven, but what about staying out of the poorhouse?" Don't think like a Gnostic; don't separate the spiritual from the material. Fearing God and living righteously results in numerous blessings—some spiritual, some material. "The reward for humility and fear of the LORD is riches and honor and life" (Pro. 22:4). "The LORD does not let the righteous go hungry, but he thwarts the craving of the wicked" (10:3). "What the wicked dreads will come upon him, but the desire of the righteous will be granted" (vs. 24). "In the house of the righteous there is much treasure, but trouble befalls the income of the wicked" (15:6). The Bible is clear that God often (but not always) rewards the righteous God-fearer, not only with spiritual blessings, but also with material blessings. We don't want to preach a prosperity gospel, yet at the same time we don't want to overreact to such preaching and espouse an unbiblical "poverty gospel" at the opposite end of the spectrum, either. Practically speaking, this means that one of the best things you can do to help your small business prosper is to seek first God's kingdom and God's righteousness every morning through Bible reading and prayer.

Another principle for acquiring wealth is to get wisdom, knowledge, and understanding. "Blessed is the one who finds wisdom, and the one who gets understanding, for the gain from her is better than gain from silver and her profit better than gold. She is more precious than jewels, and nothing you desire can compare with her. Long life is in her right hand; in her left hand are riches and honor" (3:13-16). Wisdom is better than wealth; yet acquiring wisdom usually results in acquiring some measure of wealth. As in Proverbs 3, wisdom is personified as a woman in Proverbs 8, as well, and she says, "'Riches and honor are with me, enduring wealth and righteousness'" (8:18). This may be stating the obvious, but to get wisdom and understanding one must learn to think well, to be diligent in studying. On one occasion a high school student was complaining about math. "Why am I studying this? I'll never use this after high school." I replied, "Maybe you won't, but that doesn't matter, because in the meantime you are learning to think well, and your mind is being stretched and strengthened." And I could have added, "Such thinking will most likely benefit you financially someday."

Third, we acquire wealth by tithing. "Honor the LORD with your wealth and with the firstfruits of all your produce; then your barns will be filled with plenty, and your vats will be bursting with wine" (3:9-10). Studies have shown that 17% of Americans claim to tithe, but when you actually compare the giving to earning ratio, the results reveal that only 6% actually do tithe. As a result of this rampant disobedience, our barns are empty and our wine cellars are bare. In the vernacular of our day, our paychecks are not what they might otherwise be; our labor is not being blessed. We are forfeiting blessings—spiritual and material—that God would like to bring our way. As the old adage goes, put your money where your mouth is. It's one thing to say, "He is Lord"; it's another to give him 10% of your income.

Before we continue on with three more biblical principles for how to acquire wealth, let's remember that as the heavens are higher than the earth, so are God's ways higher than our ways. Many of the principles for acquiring wealth that are in the Bible will not be found in secular manuals for amassing your fortune. For example, such manuals are completely oblivious to the connection between the fear of God and the finances of man. As in all areas of the Christian life, we are to live by faith and not by sight. How we go about acquiring our wealth is a good place to test ourselves to see whether or not we are living by faith. Clearly, living by faith is not some ethereal requirement for the people of God that doesn't relate to everyday life.

A fourth principle for acquiring wealth is to be generous—especially toward the poor. "One gives freely, yet grows all the richer; another withholds what he should give, and only suffers want. Whoever brings blessing will be enriched, and one who waters will himself be watered" (Pro. 11:24-25). John Bunyan stated it well in his classic book *Pilgrim's Progress,* which I will paraphrase: "There was a man, some thought mad, the more he gave the more he had." God not only blesses us when we give to Him, He also blesses us when we give to others.

In the Sermon on the Mount, Jesus assumes we will give alms. He said, "'Thus, when you give to the needy, sound no trumpet before you, as the hypocrites do in the synagogues and in the streets, that they may be praised by others. Truly, I say to you, they have received their reward. But when you give to the needy, do not let your left hand know what your right hand is doing, so that your giving may be in secret. And your Father who sees in secret will reward you'" (Matt. 6:2-4). When we give to the poor appropriately, which means quietly and secretly, God promises to reward us for our generosity. And there is no reason to over-spiritualize the reward of God.

Earlier I said that God rewards us when we give to Him and when we give to others. This may be a false dichotomy, because when we give to others, especially to the poor or fellow Christians, we are giving to God Himself. "Whoever is generous to the poor lends to the LORD, and he will repay him for his deed" (Pro. 19:17). When God providentially places a poor person in our path, He is placing before us an opportunity for His blessing or His cursing. "Whoever gives to the poor will not want, but he who hides his eyes will get many a curse" (28:27). John Calvin took giving to the poor seriously. At his church they took two offerings every Lord's Day. The first offering was tithes for the ministry of the church, and the second offering was for the poor and needy in their church and community. As Christians it would be great if we were known for our generosity. Besides, Jesus said, '"It is more blessed to give than to receive"' (Acts 20:35).

I hope this next point for acquiring wealth is obvious—work hard. "A slack hand causes poverty, but the hand of the diligent makes rich" (Pro. 10:4). We need to work hard—God's way—which means not being greedy for gain in the process, or walking over people in the cutthroat business world. When Abraham's and Lot's herdsmen started fighting over the land, Abraham didn't think that he had to use his authority or power to quash Lot so he could get ahead; rather he was gracious and let Lot have the land he wanted. I'm afraid that sometimes we behave like little children. What happens when two kids come home from school, and there is only one cookie left on the plate? All-out war, just as in the marketplace.

Part of working hard, of course, involves the workplace. One of the best ways to get ahead at work is to please the boss. Who's your boss? God is. Paul said, "Slaves, obey your earthly masters with fear and trembling, with a sincere heart, as you would for Christ, not by the way of eye-service, as people-pleasers, but as servants of Christ, doing the will of God from the heart, rendering service with a good will as to the Lord and not to man, knowing that whatever good anyone does, this he will receive back from the Lord, whether he is a slave or free" (Eph. 6:5-8). Regardless of your vocation you are serving the Lord, and He promises to pay you back for what you have done. This means that you don't have to work excessive hours to acquire wealth. "Do not toil to acquire wealth; be discerning enough to desist"

(Pro. 23:4). It is vain to rise early and go to bed late for more money (Ps. 127:2). Also, remember that in God's economy, six days of work with His blessing will prove to be more profitable than seven without it.

Finally, repent of all known sin. "Whoever conceals his transgressions will not prosper, but he who confesses and forsakes them will obtain mercy" (Pro. 28:13). Once again, we are reminded that the spiritual and material are woven together. Therefore, repentance is necessary for fellowship with the Lord, as well as success in business.

19

THE PURSUIT OF PEACE

It's Mandatory, Not Optional, for the People of God

Will and Ariel Durant wrote in their 1968 book *The Lessons of History*, "War is one of the constants of history, and has not diminished with civilization and democracy. In the last 3,421 years of recorded history only 268 have seen no war."[24] Doing the math, this means we experience war 92.2% of the time. Here in the United States, our nation is at war this very moment (March of 2010) in more than one country (Afghanistan and Iraq). How will we ever experience peace?

Actress Shirley MacLaine thinks she has the answer. Christian evangelist/apologist Ravi Zacharias said he was being interviewed on a television show once and the host said, "Shirley MacLaine says the sooner we get rid of the categories of good and evil, the sooner we'll experience peace. What do you think?" Ravi responded, "Why not war, unless peace is a good thing. And if it is then I don't understand the question."

Here's another brilliant suggestion for bringing about world peace that I'm sure most of you have seen, because it's on bumper stickers everywhere: "Visualize World Peace." I like the spoof on this: "Visualize Whirled Peas." I'd like to respond to the world peace bumper sticker with one of my own: "I did; now we're in Afghanistan and Iraq." Peace will not come about because we dream about it, or because we really, really, really want it to happen.

The cold, harsh reality is that sometimes we have to fight for peace, so don't prematurely beat your spears into pruning hooks. Peter admonishes Christians, "Whoever desires to love life and see good days...let him turn away from evil and do good; let him seek peace and pursue it" (1 Pet. 3:10-11). Whether we're talking about peace between nations or between individuals, we must be aggressive—we must *seek* peace and *pursue* it, because it doesn't just happen by hoping against all hope that it will come about.

The book of Proverbs places a high premium on peace. "Better is a dry morsel with quiet [peace and quiet, NIV] than a house full of feasting with strife" (Pro. 17:1). Peace is a gift from God. Just about every epistle in the New Testament begins similarly to how Romans begins: "Grace to you and peace from God our Father and the Lord Jesus Christ" (Rom. 1:7). Biblical peace is much more than the absence of conflict and much more than a cease-fire; it is wellness and wholeness, which can be experienced even when bullets are flying over our heads, or when our family has perished. After Horatio Spafford's four daughters drowned at sea in 1873, he penned these words, which became the lyrics of the hymn "It Is Well with My Soul": "When peace, like a river, attendeth my way; When sorrows like sea billows roll; Whatever my lot, Thou hast taught me to say; It is well, it is well with my soul." Peace in the midst of this kind of tragedy can only be attributed to God's goodness and grace.

Hebrews 12:14 says, "Strive for peace with everyone..." It may not always be possible, since peace is a two-way street and others may not want to be at peace with us; nevertheless we must do our part to potentially achieve peace with everyone. In the church, however, peace is not optional. "Irreconcilable differences" may be the law of the land, but it is not the law of God. Matthew 18:15-17 shows us that God demands reconciliation, or else. You say, "Or else what?" Or else you can't be a part of the church. Or else you will be treated like a tax collector. This is how serious peace in the body of Christ is to God.

To illustrate the importance of peace between brothers, Jesus said, "'So if you are offering your gift at the altar and there remember that your brother has something against you, leave your gift there before the altar and go. First be reconciled to your brother, and then come and offer your gift'" (Matt. 5:23-24). For the Jews of Jesus' day, offering your gift at the altar was at the heart of worship. God demanded these offerings for atonement. But God doesn't want them, if brothers are feuding.

Proverbs 26:17 says, "Whoever meddles in a quarrel not his own is like one who takes a passing dog by the ears." This proverb needs to be harmonized with Jesus' words, "'Blessed are the peacemakers, for they shall be called sons of God'" (Matt. 5:9). Note carefully, Jesus didn't say, "blessed are the peace*keepers*," but "blessed are the peace-*makers*." Peacekeepers are passive, while peacemakers are active. Peacekeepers stay clear of trouble. They watch the action from the sidelines, where it's safe, and lament to those around them, "Why can't we all just get along?" On the other hand, peacemakers get involved in the fight. They run out onto the playing field, where a person could get hurt, and boldly say, "Knock it off! We're going to sit down and work through this like mature Christians." It takes courage to be a peacemaker. And don't forget that Jesus Christ was willing to lay down His life, so that we could enjoy peace with God.

20

HOW TO ANSWER A FOOL

If a Fool Is Even to Be Answered in the First Place

Due to the escalation in the number of fools in America that has been occurring for far too long now, it is incumbent upon us as wise Christians to think through how we will answer this growing multitude that despises God and scorns His law. God's Word assists us in this endeavor: "Answer not a fool according to his folly, lest you be like him yourself. Answer a fool according to his folly, lest he be wise in his own eyes" (Pro. 26:4-5). Verse 4 forbids us to answer a fool according to his folly, but in the very next verse we're exhorted to answer a fool according to his folly. The apparent contradiction is easily explained, when you look at the different reasons that govern each command.

In the first instance, we shouldn't give an answer, if in doing so we will only join the fool and become fools ourselves. Unfortunately, most of us have had the regretful experience of allowing ourselves to get entangled into foolish arguments where we looked just as foolish as the person we were arguing with. Sometimes silence is more powerful than any verbal response we might give. Jesus knew how to wield silence. Matthew describes Jesus' courtroom appearance: "But when [Jesus] was accused by the chief priests and elders, he gave no answer. Then Pilate said to him, 'Do you not hear how many things they testify against you?' But he gave him no answer, not even to a single charge, so that the governor was greatly amazed" (Matt. 27:12-14).

When it comes to talking with fools we need great discernment, because fools aren't necessarily stupid. In fact, some of them are quite cunning, and they will use their intellect to trap us. On a recent political talk show a conservative guest was asked a question like this by a liberal fool (this wasn't the question, but it was this *type* of question): "Have you stopped beating your wife?" If you answer that question, *at all*, you're in trouble. The best answer here is no answer.

However, there are other situations in which no answer would be seen as a concession to the fool. The fool would be able to say, "Aha, see, he has no reply. He knows I'm right." In this case, the fool would be wise in his own eyes. "This," Solomon says, "can't be allowed to happen." This fool needs to be answered. Nineteenth century vicar Charles Bridges wrote, "(H)ere our words should be sharp as rods. The fool's back needs them. Such was Job's answer to his wife; grave, convincing, silencing—'Thou speakest as one of *the foolish* women speaketh. What! Shall we receive good at the hand of God, and shall we not receive evil?'" (Job 2:9-10).[25] Do you remember the context of this rebuke? Mrs. Job had recently lost all 10 of her children. Now her husband is on his deathbed with boils. You might be thinking, "Doesn't she deserve a little compassion?" Of course she does, but, we have to be honest—she crossed the line when she said to her husband, "Curse God and die." Consequently, Job could not let his wife go unanswered, otherwise she would have wrongly concluded that she was justified in calling upon Job to curse God for all that was happening to them.

The goal of Proverbs 26:4 is for our silence to be rebuking, while the goal of verse 5 is for our rebuke to be silencing.

In either case, we are responding as we are, not because we are trying to win an argument or outwit the other person, but because we are seeking to win him or her over to the truth.

When it comes to answering fools with sharps rods, as a result of their folly, I believe the average evanjellyfish is spineless. It seems that we have become more concerned with being politically correct than with being biblically correct. Too often we're nicer than God. If you think this is an exaggeration, consider how we address homosexuality. We say—maybe—if we even have the courage to speak at all about such a volatile issue, "The gay lifestyle is opposed to God's commands." Or, perhaps if we're feeling really bold, "Homosexuality is a sin." Now compare our comments with God's. He says unambiguously, in Leviticus 18:22, "'You shall not lie with a male as with a woman; it is an abomination.'" I can't help but wonder how many Christians would counsel the Almighty to tone down His harsh rhetoric.

Janet L. Folger wrote in *The Criminalization of Christianity*, "(O)ne night I was watching C-Span. It was airing a conference of the Human Rights Campaign, the largest homosexual lobby in the country. One of their directors, a lesbian, was pounding on the podium, screaming words I will never forget: 'We must do away with words like *abomination*!'"[26] But we must not, for although it is a fighting word, sure to get a reaction, sure to be called hate-speech, it is still God's commentary on homosexuality. God's unaltered Word always provides the best answers for fools, lest they be wise in their own eyes.

21

Pride and Humility

Those Who Walk in Pride God Is Able to Humble

In the 1990s MTV ran a program—you're going to find this hard to believe—about the "Theology of Sin." The special revolved around the "Seven Deadly Sins." In case you don't know, the so-called Seven Deadly Sins, compiled by medieval church leaders, are greed, lust, anger, envy, gluttony, sloth, and pride. As you might expect, MTV portrayed these sins as anything but deadly. In fact, by the time the program was over, from what I gleaned about the show off the Internet, it seemed that the Seven Deadly Sins were really the Seven *Desirable* Sins.[27]

In this program, sound bites were provided by different celebrities, rockers, rappers, and the ubiquitous mall rat, who voiced their opinion about these sins. For example, Queen Latifah, a rap singer/actress, said, "Pride is a sin? I wasn't aware of that!" Actress Kirstie Alley took it a step further: "I don't think pride is a sin, and I think some idiot made that up." A rocker from the group Aerosmith said, "Lust is what I live for; it's what I got into the band for—little girls in the front row." Rapper Ice-T said, "Pride is mandatory. That is one of the problems of the inner city; kids don't have enough pride. I got into a gang because of pride" (If Ice-T's logic escapes you, you're not alone).

Kurt Loder, the narrator, said at the beginning of the show that "we are dealing with compulsions." He went on to say, "The Seven Deadly Sins are not evil acts, but rather universal human compulsions that can be troubling *and highly enjoyable*." The special ended by proclaiming, "The real danger of sin is anything that does damage to your ego." "And no sin," according to MTV, "is as evil as the killjoy attitude of those who think sin is an absolute standard that offends a holy God." So there is MTV's conclusion about sin: The worst evil in all the world is that of Christianity.

The warning of Isaiah 5:20 is apropos: "Woe to those who call evil good and good evil, who put darkness for light and light for darkness, who put bitter for sweet and sweet for bitter!" The antithesis that exists between the teaching of Scripture and that of our pop culture, especially concerning pride, couldn't be more stark. James 4:6, quoting Proverbs 3:34 from the Septuagint, says, "'God opposes the proud, but gives grace to the humble.'"

Speaking of pride, C.S. Lewis wrote in *Mere Christianity*, "Well, now, we have come to the centre. According to Christian teachers, the essential vice, the utmost evil, is Pride. Unchastity, anger, greed, drunkenness, and all that, are mere fleabites in comparison: it was through Pride that the devil became the devil: Pride leads to every other vice: it is the complete anti-God state of mind."[28] Think about Lewis' comment: It was due to pride that the Day Star fell and became the devil. Isaiah 14:12-15 describes his fall. Notice the infamous five "I will" statements:

> "How you are fallen from heaven, O Day Star, son of Dawn! How you are cut down to the ground, you who laid the nations low! You said in your heart,

'I will ascend to heaven; above the stars of God I will set my throne on high; I will sit on the mount of assembly in the far reaches of the north; I will ascend above the heights of the clouds; I will make myself like the Most High.' But you are brought down to Sheol, to the far reaches of the pit."

The devil's condemnation was a result of his pride. Here's one application for the church today: An elder "must not be a recent convert, or he may become puffed up with conceit and fall into the condemnation of the devil" (1 Tim. 3:6).

The author of Proverbs warns us: "Pride goes before destruction, and a haughty spirit before a fall" (Pro. 16:18). Consider King Nebuchadnezzar: He was walking on the roof of the royal palace in Babylon, and said, "'Is not this great Babylon, which I have built by my mighty power as a royal residence and for the glory of my majesty?'" (Dan. 4:30). "While the words were still in the king's mouth, there fell a voice from heaven, 'O King Nebuchadnezzar, to you it is spoken: The kingdom has departed from you… And you shall be made to eat grass like an ox…until you know that the Most High rules the kingdom of men and gives it to whom ever he will'" (vv. 31-32). After seven years, Nebuchadnezzar repented and acknowledged that "'those who walk in pride he is able to humble'" (vs. 37).

In the New Testament we read about King Herod: "On an appointed day Herod put on his royal robes, took his seat upon the throne, and delivered an oration to them. And the people were shouting, 'The voice of a god, and not of a man!' Immediately an angel of the Lord struck him down, because he did not give God the glory, and he was eaten by worms and breathed his last" (Acts 12:21-23). The Bible concurs with the medieval fathers that pride is indeed a deadly sin.

Do you want a sad and sobering thought? Pride is a sin that we share with the devil, and we struggle with it a lot more than we realize. Moreover, pride is a fountainhead sin, because as C.S. Lewis has said, it leads to every other vice. It leads to impatience at a restaurant: "I deserve better service." It leads to rebellion in children: "My parents should let me do what I want." It causes parents to be angry with their children: "You're embarrassing me." It can result in depression, because you didn't make the team, or the grade; or you didn't get the promotion. This depression manifests itself in a black-tie self-pity party that was provoked by pride. These are just a few examples out of hundreds that we could have mentioned.

Think especially of how pride destroys relationships. King Saul could not have asked for a braver or more loyal or more dedicated or more gifted servant than David. David never let the king down. He always spoke respectfully to and of Saul. So why was Saul so hostile toward David? Why did he try to kill him on more than one occasion? The answer is found in 1 Samuel 18:7-9. After David achieved great victories for Saul, "the women sang to one another as they celebrated, 'Saul has struck down his thousands, and David his ten thousands.' And Saul was very angry, and this saying displeased him. He said, 'They have ascribed to David ten thousands, and to me they have ascribed thousands [read: *only* thousands], and what more can he have but the kingdom?' And Saul eyed David from that day on." Contrast David and Saul with David and Jonathan, Saul's son. David and Jonathan were basically best friends. Since Jonathan was Saul's oldest son he was the rightful heir to the throne, yet he knew God was going to give it to David, and yet we don't detect even a hint of jealousy on Jonathan's part. It never had a negative impact upon their relationship, due to Jonathan's humility and love for David. I can't help but wonder how many relationships in our churches are hindered by pride?

C.S. Lewis helps us understand why pride has such an adverse effect upon relationships. He wrote, "Now what you want to get clear is that Pride is *essentially* competitive—is competitive by its very nature—while the other vices are competitive only, so to speak, by accident. Pride gets no pleasure out of having something, only out of having more of it than the next man. We say that people are proud of being rich, or clever, or good-looking, but they are not. They are proud of being richer, or cleverer, or better-looking than others. If everyone else became equally rich, or clever, or good-looking there would be nothing to be proud about. It is the comparison that makes you proud: the pleasure of being above the rest. Once the element of competition has gone, pride has gone."[29]

Here's another facet that makes pride a difficult issue to address: It can make you do the right things, but with the wrong motives. Disciplining children may be the right thing to do, but not because unruly children will make you look bad as a parent. You discipline your children because God commands you to do so, for the benefit of your children. Kids are discerning; they know whether you're disciplining them out of pride or humble love.

Since we can't see a person's heart and infallibly ascertain what motivates the person to do what he or she does, we need to exercise caution when we judge his or her spiritual condition. In the first century most of the Jews revered the Pharisees as the most spiritual people they knew. The Pharisees regularly went to synagogue for services. They tithed even on their tiny spices. They prayed long and public prayers. They gave to the poor, which they announced with trumpets. They did all this, and much more; why? Pride—they loved the approval and admiration of men.

To balance the previous point, we should note that there are things that will be perceived by others as arrogant even though they aren't, such as having strong convictions. G.K. Chesterton, in his 1909 book *Orthodoxy*, stated it well: "(W)hat we suffer from to-day is humility in the wrong place.

Modesty has moved from the organ of ambition. Modesty has settled upon the organ of conviction; where it was never meant to be. A man was meant to be doubtful about himself, but undoubting about the truth; this has been exactly reversed."[30]

Well, how can we discern the motives of our own hearts? To quote Lewis again, "Luckily, we have a test. Whenever we find that our religious life is making us feel that we are good—above all, that we are better than someone else—I think we may be sure that we are being acted on, not by God, but by the devil. The real test of being in the presence of God, is that you either forget about yourself altogether or see yourself as a small, dirty object. It is better to forget about yourself altogether."[31]

22

Proverbs on Politics

What Should the Citizens Do to Turn America Around?

On January 23, 1996, Pastor Joe Wright opened a session of the Kansas House with this prayer: "Heavenly Father, we come before you today to ask Your forgiveness and to seek Your direction and guidance. We know Your Word says, 'Woe to those who call evil good,' but that is exactly what we have done. We have lost our spiritual equilibrium and reversed our values... We have exploited the poor and called it the lottery... We have rewarded laziness and called it welfare. We have killed our unborn and called it choice. We have shot abortionists and called it justifiable. We have neglected to discipline our children and called it building self-esteem. We have abused power and called it politics. We have coveted our neighbor's possessions and called it ambition. We have polluted the air with profanity and pornography and called it freedom of expression. We have ridiculed the time-honored values of our forefathers and called it enlightenment… Cleanse us from every sin and set us free… (I)n the name of Your Son, the living Savior, Jesus Christ, Amen!"

In response to his prayer, one member of the legislative body walked out in protest, and many others criticized the prayer. The press—surprise—called it a politically incorrect prayer. Apparently, many politicians can't handle the truth, and frankly many are boldly legislating *against* the truth.

Two books in my library represent the downward spiral of American culture. The first is Bill Bennett's book *The De-Valuing of America* (copyright 1992, 1994) and the second is Janet Folger's *The Criminalization of Christianity* (copyright 2005). If you think the title of her book is an overstatement, you haven't been paying attention. Consider five examples of how Christianity is a crime in this country.[32]

First, prayer is being outlawed. Verbal organized prayer offered in a school is unconstitutional, even if that prayer is both voluntary and denominationally neutral (*Engel v. Vitale*, 1962; *Abington v. Schempp*, 1963; *Commissioner of Education v. School Committee of Leyden*, 1971). If a student prays over his or her lunch, it is unconstitutional for him or her to pray out loud (*Reed v. Van Hoven*, 1965).

Second, Jesus is outlawed. A city council meeting can have prayer, as long as the persons praying do not say the name of Jesus (*Rubin v. City of Burbank*, 1999). The decision said nothing about swearing with Jesus' name.

Third, the Bible is outlawed. In Omaha, Nebraska, a student was prohibited from reading his Bible silently during his free time, or even to open his Bible at school (*Gierke v. Blotzer*, 1989). It is unconstitutional for a classroom library to contain books that deal with Christianity, or for a teacher to be seen with a personal copy of the Bible at school during school hours (*Roberts v. Madigan*, 1990).

Fourth, Christmas is outlawed. A Frederick County, Maryland, school employee was prohibited from handing out Christmas cards on a public-school campus. Red poinsettias were banned from the Ramsey Courthouse in St. Paul, Minnesota, because they offended one person who believed the flowers to be a symbol of Christianity. In Worthington, Ohio, students were prohibited from bringing in Christmas cookies with the colors red and green or in the shapes of stars or bells.

Fifth, crosses are outlawed. It is unconstitutional for a war memorial to be erected in the shape of a cross (*Lowe v. City of Eugene*, 1969). In June 2004, the Los Angeles County Supervisors voted three to two to remove a tiny cross from the official county seal rather than face a potential lawsuit from the ACLU. The cross had been there for forty-seven years. Yes, some of these cases are in isolated places, but they are nevertheless establishing precedence.

How can we reverse this trend? If God is going to bless America, then we, the people, need to repent. Before we come down on our rulers, we must be clear about why God has given us such corrupt rulers in the first place. Proverbs 28:2 tells us: "When a land transgresses, it has many rulers, but with a man of understanding and knowledge, its stability will long continue." "Many rulers" could refer to a government that places more and more bureaucrats over the people to harass them—take their money…land…children…freedom. Or "many rulers" could indicate a government in constant turmoil, so that every few months another coup takes place, leaving the land with no peace and stability. Either way, notice that the reason for "many rulers" is the transgression of the land (i.e., the people). These harsh rulers are a sign of God's judgment for the sin of the people. If the people want better leaders they must repent before they vote.

Considering What Kings and Rulers Need to Reign

What kind of leaders should we vote for? Democrats, Republicans, or Independents? Conservatives, liberals, or moderates? The Bible causes us to think in different categories altogether.

Above all, we want *wise* politicians in office. In Proverbs 8 we have the personification of wisdom, which is a picture of Jesus Christ. Wisdom says, "'When he established the heavens, I was there…when he marked out the foundations of the earth, then I was beside him, like a master workman, I was daily his delight, rejoicing before him always, rejoicing in his inhabited world and delighting in the children of man '" (vv. 27, 29b-31). Now if we back up a few verses we read, "'I, wisdom, dwell with prudence, and I find knowledge and discretion…. By me kings reign, and rulers decree what is just; by me princes rule, and nobles, all who govern justly'" (vv. 12, 15-16). Kings, rulers, princes, nobles, presidents, senators, governors, and mayors are to rule by wisdom. We want wise rulers and not stupid rulers. Initially everybody agrees with this, until we press a little further and ask, "What wisdom are we talking about?" "Where does this wisdom originate?" If a Christian were to answer honestly these days it would almost certainly be political suicide. Imagine a Supreme Court nominee being asked, "Will you uphold the Constitution of the U.S.?" And he or she responds, "Absolutely…insofar as it doesn't deviate to the right or to the left of the Word of God and the wisdom incarnate in Jesus Christ." His or her political career would suddenly come to a screeching halt.

Our first President George Washington stated, "It is impossible to govern without God and the Bible."

In his diary dated February 22, 1756, John Adams wrote, "Suppose a nation in some distant region should take the Bible for their only law-book, and every member should regulate his conduct by the precepts there exhibited! Every member would be obliged, in conscience, to temperance and frugality and industry; to justice and kindness and charity towards his fellow men; and to piety, love, and reverence, towards Almighty God... What a [Utopia]; what a Paradise would this region be!" Our second President didn't entertain the idea of a government detached from God's Word, but dreamed of the possibilities of a nation living in accordance with the Scriptures.

On July 4, 1821, John Quincy Adams declared, "The highest glory of the American Revolution was this: it connected in one indissoluble bond the principles of civil government with the principles of Christianity... From the day of the Declaration...[Americans] were bound by the laws of God, which they all, and by the laws of the Gospel, which they nearly all, acknowledge as the rules of their conduct."

The only reason why we're debating whether or not America was founded upon the principles of Christianity and the wisdom of the Bible is because we're ignorant of history. Also, the secular historians have worked hard to censor what in their view are the offensive, politically incorrect Christian references. For example: "The Mayflower Compact is depicted solely as a political document with its more striking religious elements censored out. Here is the document as presented by the textbook company. The **[boldface]** portions are missing from the textbook version: 'In the name of God, Amen. We whose names are underwritten, **the loyal subjects of our dread sovereign lord, King James, by the grace of God, of Great Britain, France, and Ireland, King, Defender of the Faith, etc.,** having undertaken **for the glory of God and advancement of the Christian faith and honor of our king and country,** a voyage to plant the first colony in the northern parts of Virginia, do **by these presents** solemnly and in the presence of God, and one another, covenant and combine ourselves together into a civil body politic...'"[33] After being taught the edited version of the Mayflower Compact, the students are tested: "Why did the pilgrims risk their lives to come to America?" They answer confidently, "For political freedom," and get an A. Now any Christian student who says, "No, it was primarily for the glory of God and the advancement of the Christian faith" is seen as reading his Christian bias and agenda into history, and he or she fails.

Many today would be up in arms over Washington's statement that it is impossible to govern without God and the Bible. Of course conversion cannot be legislated, but does it necessarily follow that the laws of the land shouldn't be based on God's Word? We only have two alternatives before us: We will either be governed by Christian laws (i.e., biblical laws) or by secular laws; the laws of God or the laws of man. Our founding fathers saw this; why don't our present leaders—including most of the so-called conservatives?

Legislating Morality

If we're going to talk about politics, we need to talk about morality. Perhaps you've heard it said that you can't legislate morality. If you couldn't legislate morality, you couldn't legislate—period. Every piece of legislation is a reflection of somebody's morality. Laws are not morally neutral. The question is not *whether* politicians will legislate morality, but *what* (or whose) morality they will legislate.

R.C. Sproul Jr. made the astute observation that "in the Old Testament you find an example of the executive branch, as well as the judicial branch, but you don't find the legislative branch. Why? Because God Himself gave the people the laws by which they were to be governed."

Let me ask you, "Is homosexuality wrong?" And here's the follow-up question: "Why is it wrong?" Yes it is wrong, and it is wrong for only one reason: God has told us in His Word that it is wrong. Actually He states it stronger than that, as I said earlier, but I think you get the point. It's time for Christians to stop being ambiguous as to why certain practices or lifestyles are right or wrong. For example, we need to stop talking about "family values." With the current redefinition of marriage and family, couldn't somebody be in favor of Bill and Bob's loving, homosexual family values? "Family values" is quickly becoming a meaningless reference for Christians to use. Nor do we want to talk about "traditional values." Many progressives and evolutionists despise tradition. Not that we care, but is something right just because it's been around for a long time? In some cultures polygamy is a tradition. In others, cannibalism is. In our own culture abortion is now a tradition, and many argue in favor of upholding *Roe v. Wade*, because it's part of our legal tradition. Lawyers call this precedence.

Why has pornography been legalized? Why has school prayer been outlawed? Why has abortion been legalized? Why do homosexuals have special rights? Because we have rulers who have been legislating *morality* apart from and contrary to the wisdom of God's Word. Thus, without biblical absolutes and principles to guide and govern us, we are left to the mercy of the prosperous, the powerful, and the perverse.

If God is going to bless America, we need righteous rulers. "It is an abomination to kings to do evil, for the throne is established by righteousness" (Pro. 16:12). Simply put, character counts. King Lemuel was counseled by his mother: "Do not give your strength to women, your ways to those who destroy kings. It is not for kings, O Lemuel, it is not for kings to drink wine, or for rulers to take strong drink, lest they drink and forget what has been decreed and pervert the rights of all the afflicted" (Pro. 31:3-5). Rulers are not to be womanizers or drunkards. Are any mental images coming to mind? It's interesting that voting guides for churches tell you about the positions of each candidate on certain issues, but nothing about the candidate's character. Doesn't character matter? Leaders lacking in character should be rejected, or voted out of office—even if they represent your policies.

I'm sure many of you are wrestling with my last statement, but remember Solomon? He was the wisest ruler ever, yet his character eroded over time. Kings were forbidden to acquire many horses and chariots, as well as to have many wives and excessive accumulations of silver and gold (Deut. 17:14-17). Yet Solomon was unrestrained and had 40,000 stalls of horses for his chariots (1 Kgs. 4:26). "He had 700 wives, princesses, and 300 concubines. And his wives turned away his heart" (1 Kgs. 11:3). Also, "the weight of gold that came to Solomon in one year was 666 talents of gold" (2 Chr. 9:13). As a result of Solomon's self-indulgence, the Lord became angry with Solomon and tore away most of the kingdom from him. Furthermore, the Lord raised up enemies who fought against Israel (1 Kgs. 11:9-14). The end result was that the whole nation suffered due to the king's unrighteous life.

One final word: If God is going to bless America, we need faithful judges. In a word, we need justice. "By justice a king builds up the land, but he who exacts gifts tears it down" (Pro. 29:4). Bribes of course pervert justice. "The wicked accepts a bribe in secret to pervert the ways of justice" (17:23).

Proverbs 17:15 warns: "He who justifies the wicked and he who condemns the righteous are both alike an abomination to the LORD." Lady Justice is supposed to be blindfolded so she can't see one's economic state or race or creed. Unfortunately, the poor often have trouble getting a fair trial, while the wealthy get away with murder. The poor, who can't afford high-priced attorneys, especially need to receive justice. Faithful justice for the poor establishes the king's throne forever (29:14).

23

Shepherding a Child's Heart

Dealing with the Core of Our Children's Being

It's been said quaintly, and accurately, that the heart of the problem is the problem of the heart. If you have any doubts about the validity of that statement, read Jeremiah 17:9-10a: "The heart is deceitful above all things, and desperately sick; who can understand it? 'I the Lord search the heart.'" If God is interested in anything, He is interested in the condition of our hearts. '"For the Lord sees not as man sees: man looks on the outward appearance, but the Lord looks on the heart'" (1 Sam. 16:7).

Some time ago one of our elders had a heart attack. His doctor said to him, "You look too healthy to be in the hospital; what are you doing here?" Our elder looked as healthy as a horse on the outside, but that was irrelevant, because what mattered most was the condition of his heart. What's true for the physical realm is equally true for the spiritual realm. Jesus blasted the Pharisees and scribes, '"You hypocrites! Well did Isaiah prophesy of you, when he said: "This people honors me with their lips, but their heart is far from me; in vain do they worship me, teaching as the commandments of men" ' " (Matt. 15:7-9).

Explaining the importance of the heart, Jesus stated, "'But what comes out of the mouth proceeds from the heart, and this defiles a person. For out of the heart come evil thoughts, murder, adultery, sexual immorality, theft, false witness, slander. These are what defile a person'" (vv. 18-20a). Everything about us flows from the heart. Therefore, above all things, God is concerned about our hearts. Likewise as parents, we should be primarily interested in capturing and shepherding the hearts of our children.

The burden of the father in Proverbs 23:26 is for the heart of his son. He pleads, "My son, give me your heart." Why does he want his child's heart? Because if he has his son's heart, he has his son's love, life, and loyalty. Incidentally, this is why God wants our hearts, because He wants our love, life, and loyalty. Therefore, we should view parenting not simply as providing for our children, so that they have food, clothing, shelter, and a good education. We should think of parenting as shepherding our children's hearts. We want to deal with the core of their being. As we nurture the hearts of our children, we're affecting that which is the wellspring of their life. So how do we shepherd a child's heart?

For starters, we need to protect the child's heart from evil influences. "Keep your heart with all vigilance, for from it flow the springs of life" (Pro. 4:23). The New American Standard Bible translates this verse, "*Watch* over your heart..." "*Guard* your heart" would be a good translation. The picture in the Hebrew Scriptures is of a garrison of soldiers surrounding the heart to protect it from the enemy. Until children are wiser and mature enough to do this for themselves, their parents must assume this responsibility.

One time I was talking with a mother who took her children out of the government school, because of the destructive influences. I said, "Oh, so you're sheltering your children."

She responded defensively, "Oh, no, I'm just..." After she hemmed and hawed for a minute, I jumped in to rescue her, saying, "Yes, you are, and you don't have to apologize." When did it become wrong for parents to shelter their children from disgusting, demonic, disturbing, and destructive forces? Isn't that what we're supposed to be doing as parents? If you've ever been accused of being overprotective, wear that accusation like a badge of honor. But if I can speak frankly, being *over*protective is hardly the problem in the average evangelical household. The vast majority of parents need to be more vigilant about the movies, music, Internet sites, video games, friends, school curriculum, etc., that their children encounter on a daily basis. I hope we haven't bought into the myth of neutrality—*nothing is neutral.* Every single one of the areas just mentioned bombards our impressionable kids with certain values, philosophies, and religious persuasions.

There is an all-out assault upon our children and their hearts, which requires parents as never before to be attentive guardian shepherds. Let's not be asleep on our watch, or too busy at work, or comatose in front of the TV, while our kids are who-knows-where doing who-knows-what with who-knows-whom.

You know there is a real problem in our midst when television ads have to advise parents on how to be parents. Recently, I saw an ad counseling parents to talk to their kids about drugs. Some time ago there was an ad that asked parents, "Do you know where your kids are?" Parents should know where their children are at all times. If parents don't, they should relinquish the honorable title of parent.

As parents, we don't want to just be *reactive*—protecting our children from every evil influence that threatens to corrupt their hearts—although this is certainly an essential and necessary aspect of parenting. We also want to be *proactive;* we want to be intentional in the exposure our kids receive.

After lamenting the low standards and liberal agenda that permeate the government schools, we need to take action and decide what type of education we want our kids to receive. After feeling frustrated over the abundance of filth that Hollywood spews forth every year, we then need to be aggressive and thoughtful about how our children will spend their free time. So, as I said earlier, parents need not apologize for sheltering their children, yet so much more needs to be done.

Assuming that it were even possible to drive back every external enemy of our children's hearts, so that all our children's exposure were positive and wholesome, there would still be an internal issue to deal with, namely the "(f)olly [that] is bound up in the heart of a child" (Pro. 22:15a). Children have *folly* within, not sugar and spice and everything nice. Therefore, discipline is a huge part of parenting. "Folly is bound up in the heart of a child, but the rod of discipline drives it far from him" (vs. 15). Rather than disciplining according to clear, biblical commands, parents are coddling according to the latest self-esteem psychobabble. As a result, kids are out of control and they can't be taught or disciplined. Ask any teacher, "Which kids are the hardest to teach?" and without hesitation the teacher will tell you, "The ones who aren't disciplined."

Helen Keller's life illustrates the importance of discipline. As a young child she completely lost her sight and hearing. Her family members didn't discipline her, probably because they felt sorry for her. Anne Sullivan, Helen's teacher, had a hard time teaching Helen at first, because of the battle of wills that took place, in addition to the obvious handicaps. Author Alexander Strauch explains:

> "At times, [Helen] would lie on the floor, kicking and screaming. When Anne tried to discipline her, she would pinch and scream. Out of this nearly impos-

> sible situation, Anne Sullivan taught her language and love. In a letter to a friend, Anne Sullivan reveals the secret 'gateway' to educating and loving Helen: 'I suppose I shall have many such battles with the little woman before she learns the only two essential things I can teach her, obedience and love.
>
> '"I very soon made up my mind that I could do nothing with Helen in the midst of the family, who have always allowed her to do exactly as she pleased. She has tyrannized everybody...and like all tyrants she holds tenaciously to her divine right to do as she pleases... I saw clearly that it was useless to try to teach her language or anything else until she learned to obey me. I have thought about it a great deal, and the more I think, the more certain I am that obedience is the gate-way through which knowledge, yes, and love, too, enter the mind of the child.'
>
> "Anne Sullivan, an exceptionally gifted teacher, understood the significance of obedience in the process of education. She saw the connection between obedience and love."[34]

If I were to boil down my parental objectives to only two, they would be to impart *love* and *knowledge* to my kids. Proverbs states that discipline plays an integral role in the accomplishment of both these objectives. First, I want my kids to feel so loved that the question of my love for them never crosses their minds. How can I fulfill this objective? By smothering them with hugs and kisses; by verbalizing my love; by reading books to them and playing games with them. And also by disciplining them. "Whoever spares the rod hates his son, but he who loves him is diligent to discipline him" (Pro. 13:24). Discipline communicates love, which a child will *eventually* understand, when he or she matures. This is imitation of our perfect, heavenly Father who '"disciplines the one he loves, and chastises every son whom he receives"' (Heb. 12:6). The only ones God doesn't discipline are those who are "illegitimate children and not sons" (vs. 8). It would be a travesty if our failure to discipline told our children they were unloved bastards.

Second, I want to give my children knowledge. I want to saturate their minds with the whole counsel of God so they will be wise Christians. "The rod and reproof give wisdom, but a child left to himself brings shame to his mother" (Pro. 29:15). Applying the board of education to the seat of learning produces wisdom. Lord willing, my kids will say with the psalmist some day, "It is good for me that I was afflicted, that I might learn your statutes" (Ps. 119:71), and "I understand more than the aged, for I keep your precepts" (119:100).

Shepherding our children demands that we be diligent to protect their hearts from evil influences, to discipline the folly that is in their hearts, and to capture their hearts through a vibrant relationship with them. I heard Christian evangelist/apologist Josh McDowell say succinctly at a conference many years ago, "Rules without relationship equals rebellion." And this relationship should include listening, communicating, and touch.

The father in Proverbs says, "My son, be attentive to my words; incline your ear to my sayings" (Pro. 4:20). We parents want our children to hang on our every word, but let's not be too distracted to return the favor. Our children long to be heard from us as well. To reiterate the words of Dr. Paul Tournier: "Listen to all the conversations of our world, between nations as well as those between couples. They, are, for the most part, *dialogues of the deaf*." One time when my daughter Lydia was about 5 years old, she was talking to me while I was focused on the computer monitor in front of me. When she realized she didn't have my undivided attention, she grabbed my face with her two little hands and turned it toward her saying, "Daddy, look at me."

Moreover, we might be surprised by what we learn when we perceptively look at our children when they talk to us. "A glad heart makes a cheerful face, but by sorrow of heart the spirit is crushed" (Pro. 15:13). A happy heart, a depressed heart, an anxious heart, or a sorrowful heart is seen in the countenance of our children. Engaged parents can read their children well, and then respond appropriately. "Whoever sings songs to a heavy heart is like one who takes off a garment on a cold day, and like vinegar on soda" (Pro. 25:20).

If we listen carefully to our children, we can then communicate with them more effectively, particularly by addressing the issues of their heart. By the way, what are the issues of your child's heart? Do you know what they are? Could you name one right now? Even a little one, such as frustration with acne or difficultly with a class he or she taking or trouble with a friend? Especially as our children grow older we have to work hard at this. "The purpose in a man's heart is like deep water, but a man of understanding will draw it out" (Pro. 20:5). If you're not familiar with your children's issues, ask questions and draw them out. My wife Michele has helped me with the art of asking good questions. I used to ask vague, general questions such as, "How was school today?" and my children would respond, "OK." My wife told me that I needed to be more specific if I wanted to get them to open up. So now I ask about their favorite class, best friends, a book's slant on a given topic, etc.

Touch and physical affection are also important. Studies have indicated that if a newborn baby is placed in isolation with physical nourishment, but no corresponding physical affection, he or she will die. Our Lord was always extending His hands to touch people, including the untouchables. Mark relays one such occasion: "And a leper came to him, imploring him, and kneeling said to him, 'If you will, you can make me clean.' Moved with pity, he stretched out his hand and touched him and said to him, 'I will; be clean'" (Mk. 1:40-41). Most likely this was the first human touch this leper had experienced in years, due to a disease that forced him to withdraw from society. Jesus listened to the concerns of this leper; He communicated reassuring words to his doubtful heart; and He also "stretched out his hand and touched him." This touch may seem like a little thing, but the Spirit of God made sure it was recorded for our instruction, because it is most certainly *not* a little thing. This is what our children need: our listening ears, our insightful words, and our physical affection. If they don't receive these from us, they will be vulnerable to those who will fill the vacuum.

In 2 Samuel 15:1-6, we read about how the insidious Absalom stole the hearts of the men of Israel. First, he would listen to their disputes. Then he would address their complaints: "'See, your claims are good and right, but there is no man designated by the king to hear you'" (vs. 3). "And whenever a man came near to pay homage to him, he would put out his hand and take hold of him and kiss him. Thus Absalom did to all of Israel who came to the king for judgment. So Absalom stole the hearts of the men of Israel" (vv. 5-6). Here's the frightening lesson: If we don't listen to our children, give them wise counsel, and show them affection, some devious Absalom will, and he will capture their hearts. So let me ask, "At this very moment, do you have your children's hearts?" "Do they want to spend time with you?" "Do they speak respectfully to you?" "Do they want to please you?" (We could ask these same questions to see if God has our hearts.) If the answer is no, we need to make the necessary corrections *immediately*.

24

The Vexation of a Fool

Learning to Ignore an Insult

"The vexation of a fool is known at once, but the prudent ignores an insult" (Pro. 12:16). Vexation is not a common word today, but in earlier eras, such as Jane Austen's (1775-1817), it was used regularly, along with one of my favorite antiquated phrases, "make haste." The verb "vex" is defined by Webster's as "to give trouble to, especially in a petty or nagging way; disturb, annoy, irritate." The New International Version translates this verse as: "A fool shows his annoyance at once, but a prudent man overlooks an insult." This proverb addresses the person who is annoyed by even the slightest irritation or inconvenience. The Bible pulls no punches; such a person is a fool.

How do we know that this fool is vexed or annoyed? Because he or she wastes no time in making this vexation known to the world through ranting and raving or pouting or letters or e-mails or phone calls, etc. I could be overly critical, but it seems that this proverb is desperately needed in our crybaby, "You hurt my feelings," "I'm a victim" culture of hypersensitive, self-absorbed whiners.

We don't have to mention any names, but there was a certain 4-year-old boy who said too often for his daddy's liking, "They hurt my feelings." Dad would follow up, "What did they do?" The little boy would answer, "They laughed at me" or "They looked at me." But let's be honest: young children aren't the only ones who are easily offended or hurt. "A receptionist for Florida Governor Jeb Bush's office came under fire for posting at her desk a greeting card showing a flag with a cross on it. A lawsuit was filed, and though the purpose of the card was to honor those who lost their lives on September 11, state senator Debbie Wasserman Schultz (D-Weston) declared, 'To me, it's offensive and hurtful.'"[35] Hurt by a greeting card, because it had a tiny cross on it? Come on!

We're so worried about hurting some child's fragile feelings or wounding his or her precious self-esteem that we now have sporting events such as peewee baseball, where keeping score is forbidden. We wouldn't want the losers to be scarred for life from the trauma, after all. Yet whom do we think we're fooling? After this supposed no-score game is over, one team is jumping up and down while the other is acting in a more subdued manner. These are great opportunities to instruct our children about life; to teach them to be humble winners and graceful losers. Our kids need to learn that often life isn't "fair." You don't always win. You don't always get the best grades. You don't always get the toys your friends have, and on and on it goes. If we don't teach these lessons to our children when they are young, we will rear a generation of easily annoyed fools.

Also, beware of becoming a victim. It will make you think that you are justified for being so vexed. Moreover, it will adversely affect your behavior. In C.S. Lewis' book, *The Lion, the Witch and the Wardrobe*, Edmund betrays his two sisters and brother, because he feels that *he* was the victim. For many years my wife and I have been repeating a maxim that I heard a pastor say: "Hurting people hurt people." We've seen this truth manifested countless times in all areas of life.

So what's the antidote? The second half of Proverbs 12:16 tells us: "but the prudent ignores an insult." Our natural, fleshly, tendency is to strike back, and to strike back with greater force, or to think of a good, witty comeback to put the person in his or her place. But what did Jesus tell us to do? He said, "'Do not resist the one who is evil. But if anyone slaps you on the right cheek, turn to him the other also'" (Matt. 5:39). We're talking about a backhanded *slap*, not a punch. This verse doesn't forbid self-defense; what it forbids is returning insult for insult.

Our Lord practiced what He preached, and He gave us an example to emulate. We read in Matthew's Gospel: "Then they spit in his face and struck him. And some slapped him, saying, 'Prophesy to us, you Christ! Who is it that struck you?'" (Matt. 26:67-68). How did Jesus respond? He could have struck them down in an instant with fire from heaven, but He was a prudent man and ignored the insults. Some want to protest, "But they shouldn't be allowed to get away with that!" Hear me loud and clear: They're not getting away with anything. Speaking of Christ's demeanor, Peter wrote, "When he was reviled, he did not revile in return; when he suffered, he did not threaten, but continued entrusting himself to him who judges justly" (1 Pet. 2:23). By entrusting Himself to the just Judge, He was leaving room for God's wrath, because He knew the Scriptures: "'Vengeance is mine, I will repay, says the Lord'" (Rom. 12:19, quoting Deut. 32:35). We should do likewise knowing that "'the LORD will vindicate his people'" (Deut. 32:36).

25

"Hope Deferred"

Dealing with Depression

In 1835 a man visited a doctor in Florence, Italy. The man was quite despondent. He was exhausted from a lack of sleep. Moreover, he couldn't eat, and he avoided his friends. The doctor examined him and found him to be in excellent physical health. The physician concluded that his patient needed to have a good time, so he recommended that he go to the circus that was in town and see its star performer, a clown named Grimaldi. Night after night Grimaldi had the people rolling in the aisles. "You must go see him," the doctor advised. "Grimaldi is the world's funniest clown. He will make you laugh and cure your sadness." "No," replied the despairing man, "he can't help me. You see, I am Grimaldi!"

We all deal with depression to varying degrees, and we all concur that it usually takes more than a visit to the circus to drive it away.

The causes of depression are myriad and complex; often they go undetected. Even "the prince of preachers" Charles Spurgeon battled depression. He was no doubt referring to personal experience, when he wrote: "Causeless depression is not to be reasoned with, nor can David's harp charm it away... [We might] (a)s well fight with the mist as with this shapeless, undefineable, yet all-beclouding hopelessness... The iron bolt which so mysteriously fastens the door of hope and holds our spirits in gloomy prison, needs a heavenly hand to push it back; and when that hand is seen we cry with the apostle, 'Blessed be God...the Father of mercies, and the God of all comfort.'"[36]

At one level, depression is a state of "all-beclouding *hopelessness*." A depressed person lacks hope. Proverbs 13:12 states: "Hope deferred makes the heart sick." Let's consider this verse from two different perspectives. The first is that of giving false hope to others. When *The Lion, the Witch and the Wardrobe* was made into a movie, I told my kids that I would take them to see it. After it was out a couple of weeks, and I still hadn't taken them, I could sense in their voices a deferred hope, when they gently reminded me that I had promised to take them. Children are usually better at keeping us accountable than our fellow adults. As an adult I'd be too embarrassed to say, "Hey, when are we going to see that movie you promised to take me to?" In fact, we are so used to being disappointed and let down that we hardly give it a second thought. This should not be the case in the Christian community. And we need to ask if we've become accustomed to letting others down. It could be as simple as saying, "Let's get together for lunch sometime," but you never do, and if the truth were known you never really intended to follow through. This can be discouraging.

The second perspective I'd like us to think about is that of giving false hope to ourselves. You might be wondering how we do that. We do it by having unrealistic expectations that are often seen in a demanding spirit. Christian psychologist Larry Crabb said, "We are a demanding people... We *demand* that spouses respond to our needs; we *demand* that our children exhibit the fruit of our godly training; we *demand* that our churches be sensitive to our concerns by providing certain ministries; we *demand* that slow drivers get out of the passing lane; we *demand* that no one hurt us again the way we were hurt before; we *demand* that legitimate pleasures, long denied, be ours to enjoy."[37] With such unrealistic expectations we are bound to be disappointed and depressed.

Crabb goes on to say, "The way God arranges things sometimes seems uniquely designed to frustrate us: a tire goes flat on the way to the hospital, the sink backs up an hour before overnight company arrives, a friend lets you down during a time when you most need support, you suddenly develop laryngitis the day of your presentation to important buyers. In times of frustration, our High Priest sometimes seems more callous to our needs than sympathetic."[38] Add God's "frowning providence," as William Cowper called it, to our demanding spirit, and we will inevitably experience "hope deferred."

If anybody could have struggled with depression it was Joseph of the Old Testament. Yet he lived his whole life with an acute awareness of God's presence, and that made all the difference. He was like the godly man who was asked shortly before his death how he handled the fact that God was allowing him to die despite the prayers of thousands for his healing. He replied, "When I am in the presence of God, it seems uniquely unbecoming to demand anything." Brothers and sisters, desire much, pray for miracles, ask for God's blessing, but demand nothing. A demanding spirit crosses the line, and just brings disappointment.

Don't Forget to Preach to Yourself

Someone has said, "We can live forty days without food, eight days without water, four minutes without air, but only a few seconds without hope." Read a typical suicide letter, and you will detect that the person was drowning in an ocean of hopelessness. To overcome depression, we must restore hope. Psalms 42 and 43 (originally one Psalm) is one man's fight to triumph over depression.

The psalmist is being agitated by his adversaries, he remembers better days filled with joy and thanksgiving, and, worst of all, he feels rejected by God. He is obviously despondent: "My tears have been my food day and night… I say to God, my rock: 'Why have you forgotten me? Why do I go about mourning...?'" (Ps. 42:3, 9). However, this man is not content to just give up and wallow in self-pity. Too many of us are wallowing. We must not give in to our emotions. Emotions can be very deceiving. They often lie to us and tell us that things are far worse than they really are. They tell us that God must not care about us. They tell us our situation is hopeless. They tell us we will never recover. They tell us to just give up. *We must not listen.*

We should question our emotions, and talk to ourselves. Some of you talk to yourself on a regular basis, and you feel a little self-conscience about it. Well, let me put you at ease. This is really a biblical thing to do. So you're OK, unless of course you start answering yourself. Notice how the psalmist deals with his discouragement by questioning himself: "Why are you downcast, O my soul? Why so disturbed within me?" He then goes on to preach to himself: "Put your hope in God, for I will yet praise him my Savior and my God" (we find this exhortation three times; Ps. 42:5, 11; 43:5 NIV).

Martyn Lloyd-Jones understood the importance of not listening to ourselves, but of talking to ourselves: "I suggest that the main trouble in this whole matter of spiritual depression in a sense is this, that we allow our self to talk to us instead of talking to our self… Have you realized that most of your unhappiness in life is due to the fact that you are listening to yourself instead of talking to yourself?… (Y)ou have to address yourself, preach to yourself, question yourself. You must say to your soul: 'Why art thou cast down'—what business have you to be disquieted? You must turn on yourself, upbraid yourself, condemn yourself, exhort yourself, and say to yourself: 'Hope thou in God'—instead of muttering in this depressed, unhappy way. And then you must go on to remind yourself of God, Who God is, and what God is and what God has done, and what God has pledged Himself to do."[39]

"Hope deferred makes the heart sick, but a desire fulfilled is a tree of life" (Pro. 13:12). Fulfilled desires put an end to hopelessness, but what do you do in the interim? You preach to yourself, specifically reminding yourself that "we know that for those who love God all things work together for good, for those who are called according to his purpose" (Rom. 8:28). This practice of preaching to oneself sustained Joseph through all that he went through. In what could be described as the Romans 8:28 of the Old Testament, Genesis 50:20, Joseph said to his brothers, when their relationship was restored, "As for you, you meant evil against me, but God meant it for good, to bring it about that many people should be kept alive, as they are today."

William Cowper, who struggled greatly with depression, was probably preaching to himself in accordance with Romans 8:28 when he wrote the poem/hymn, "God Moves in a Mysterious Way":

God moves in a mysterious way His wonders to perform;
He plants his footsteps in the sea, And rides upon the storm.

Deep in unfathomable mines Of never-failing skill,
He treasures up his bright designs And works his sovereign will.

Ye fearful saints, fresh courage take, The clouds ye so much drea

Are big with mercy, and shall break In blessings on your head.

Judge not the Lord by feeble sense, But trust him for his grace;
Behind a frowning providence He hides a smiling face.

His purposes will ripen fast, Unfolding every hour;
The bud may have a bitter taste, But sweet will be the flower.

Blind unbelief is sure to err, And scan his work in vain:
God is his own interpreter, And He will make it plain.

26

HOLINESS PROVOKES HOSTILITY

Considering Why the Righteous Are an Abomination to the Wicked

Do you sometimes feel like a foreigner in this world? In a very real way Christians are (1 Pet. 2:11). But, even more than this, do you at times also feel like a *hated* foreigner? Jesus told us not to be surprised by this hatred: "'If the world hates you, know that it has hated me before it hated you. If you were of the world, the world would love you as its own; but because you are not of the world, but I chose you out of the world, therefore the world hates you'" (Jn. 15:18-19).

Proverbs 29:27 is a fascinating verse that speaks of the natural animosity that exists between the righteous and the unrighteous: "An unjust man is an abomination to the righteous, but one whose way is straight is an abomination to the wicked." What accounts for this mutual abomination? Simply the way each side lives. A righteous man looks at the sinful lifestyle of the wicked man and finds it abominable, while the wicked man in turn looks at the holy lifestyle of the righteous man and finds it abominable.

The very first example of the wicked despising the righteous is found in Genesis 4, where Cain rises up against his own brother, Abel, and stabs him to death (Gen. 4:8). Why did Cain kill Abel? Because he hated him. And why did he hate him? John in his first letter provides us with a commentary that explains why: "We should not be like Cain, who was of the evil one and murdered his brother. And why did he murder him? Because his own deeds were evil and his brother's righteous. Do not be surprised, brothers, that the world hates you" (1 Jn. 3:12-13). Cain hated his brother, and killed him simply for being a righteous person. Abel did not preach at his brother—at least not verbally, though his life preached loudly. Nor did Abel behave in a self-righteous manner that would have justifiably irritated and annoyed his brother. All Abel did was try to humbly live a life pleasing to God. But that was too much for Cain, he couldn't tolerate such behavior, so he killed his brother.

Here is another account of animosity, albeit much less violent animus, that took place in the 1970s: "A few years ago one of the leading golfers on the professional tour was invited to play in a foursome with Gerald Ford, then president of the United States, Jack Nicklaus, and Billy Graham. The golfer was especially in awe of playing with Ford and Billy Graham (he had played frequently with Nicklaus before).

"After the round of golf was finished, one of the other pros came up to the golfer and asked, 'Hey, what was it like playing with the President and with Billy Graham?'

"The pro unleashed a torrent of cursing, and in a disgusted manner said, 'I don't need Billy Graham stuffing religion down my throat.' With that he turned on his heel and stormed off, heading for the practice tee.

"His friend followed the angry pro to the practice tee. The pro took out his driver and started to beat out balls in fury. His neck was crimson and it looked like steam was coming from his ears. His friend said nothing. He sat on a bench and watched. After a few minutes the anger of the pro was spent. He settled down. His friend said quietly, 'Was Billy a little rough on you out there?'

"The pro heaved an embarrassed sigh and said, 'No, he didn't even mention religion. I just had a bad round.'"[40]

R.C. Sproul comments: "Astonishing. Billy Graham had said not a word about God, Jesus, or religion, yet the pro had stormed away after the game accusing Billy of trying to ram religion down his throat. How can we explain this? It's really not difficult... Billy Graham is so identified with religion, so associated with the things of God, that his very presence is enough to smother the wicked man… Holiness provokes hatred. The greater the holiness, the greater the…hostility toward it. It seems insane."[41]

Sinful people repulsed by holy living may respond in a number of mean or violent ways. Christians, who are repulsed by ungodly living, must be careful not to respond in a similar manner. We are to love our enemies, pray for those who persecute us, and "not be overcome by evil, but overcome evil with good" (Rom. 12:21). Peter told his readers, "Keep your conduct among the Gentiles honorable, so that when they speak against you as evildoers, they may see your good deeds and glorify God on the day of visitation" (1 Pet. 2:12). They glorify God on the day of visitation, because the holy life of the Christian eventually convinced the unbeliever that he was wrong. Therefore, he repented and put his faith in Christ. Now, the coming of Christ causes him to glorify God instead of curse God. Never underestimate the power of a godly life.

27

Discipline Is Evangelistic

One Way to Help Save Your Child's Soul from Hell

"Folly is bound up in the heart of a child" (Pro. 22:15a). *Folly*, not goodness or innocence or ignorance. Folly can be defined as morally reprehensible behavior; it is the opposite of wisdom, which is morally righteous behavior. "Folly is bound up in the heart of a child, but the rod of discipline drives it far from him" (Pro. 22:15). God's ordained means for dealing with folly is not yelling, time-outs, grounding, taking away the TV or video games, or a year at a juvenile center; but, instead, it is the rod of discipline. This is not rocket science. This is easy to understand. The question is do we believe God or the so-called experts, who are nearly unanimous in their opposition to spanking? If we fail to drive out folly when it is relatively small and weak, it will grow like a weed, and harden like concrete, until it is almost impenetrable and impossible to break.

"Do not withhold discipline from a child" (Pro. 23:13a). Parents who refuse to discipline their children, or who are too lazy or too busy to discipline their children, are sinning. "Do not withhold discipline from a child; if you strike him with a rod, he will not die" (Pro. 23:13). This is a word to tenderhearted parents who think that spanking is cruel and unusual punishment. If I can paraphrase, God is saying, "Come on, spank the kid for his rebellion, it won't kill him."

We can take this a step further. Not only will proper discipline not kill a child, it will in fact deliver him or her from death—spiritual death. "If you strike him with the rod, you will save his soul from Sheol" (Pro. 23:14). "Sheol" is translated as "hell" in the New King James Version. This could be a reference to physical or spiritual death. I lean toward the latter since the concern is for the child's *soul.* Consider one profound implication: Discipline is evangelistic; spanking is an evangelistic tool designed to deliver your child from the pit of hell. Consider why this is.

First, discipline teaches your children that God is the ultimate authority they need to answer to. You should tell your children that you are spanking them for their sinful behavior, because that is what God commands you to do, and you have to submit to God. You are not disciplining your children because they frustrate you or anger you, but because they have sinned against God, even if it's by disrespecting or disobeying you. This teaches children that in our home we all live according to God's Word, and answer to Him.

Second, discipline teaches your children that they are sinners. Nobody cries out for forgiveness from the Savior without an acute awareness of his or her sin. Discipline is a painful reminder to children that they are sinners; they are not little angels.

Third, discipline teaches your children that sin is serious. We live in a culture that scoffs at sin. Sin is often presented as that which is tasty or fun. Your children will not suffer from such heresy if sin results in a sober, stinging spanking.

Fourth, discipline teaches your children that sin must be punished. Again, we can see that our culture is way off track. Many think that sin is no big deal, so they don't see any reason for the punishment of hell. Discipline helps children to see that God's anger toward sin needs to be propitiated, turned aside. It gives them a greater appreciation for Jesus' atoning work on the cross.

Fifth, discipline teaches your children that they need forgiveness. Discipline should include you or your child praying that God will forgive him or her for his or her sin. This shows your children that regardless of what people they have offended, first and foremost their sin offends a holy God. It should also include thanking God for the death of Christ on the cross for their sin, which makes this forgiveness possible.

Sixth, discipline teaches your children that forgiveness is real. After you spank them and pray with them, remind them that they are forgiven. The principle of 1 John 1:9 should become like second nature: "If we confess our sins, he is faithful and just to forgive us our sins and to cleanse us from all unrighteousness." And for this point to really hit home you have to treat your children as being forgiven.

Seventh, discipline teaches your children that they need God's grace to live as Christians. The final petition in the prayer with your child should be for God to help the child overcome his or her sin. This will be a practical way to instruct your child that we cannot live as God is calling us to live without us having the power of the Holy Spirit.

Let Eli be a warning to us. The LORD said, "I am about to punish his house forever, for the iniquity that he knew, because his sons were blaspheming God, and he did not restrain them. Therefore I swear to the house of Eli that the iniquity of Eli's house shall not be atoned for by sacrifice or offering forever" (1 Sam. 3:13-14).

28

The Ideal Woman

"She Is Worth Far More than Rubies"

A few years ago a newspaper ran a review of Joan Jacobs Brumberg's book *The Body Project*. John Piper comments, "The book is about the difference between how girls saw themselves 100 years ago and how they saw themselves at the end of the twentieth century. Brumberg analyzes diaries of adolescent girls from the 1830s to the 1990s. Her conclusion, according to the reviewer: 'In the nineteenth and early twentieth centuries, girls' diaries focused on 'good works' and perfecting the character. In the 1990s, the diaries are fixated on 'good looks,' on perfecting the body.

"For example, one diary from 1892 says, 'Resolved… (t)o think before speaking. To work seriously. To be self restrained in conversation and actions... To be dignified. Interest myself more in others.' Contrast this with an entry from 1982: 'I will try to make myself better in any way I possibly can with the help of my budget and baby-sitting money. I will lose weight, get new lenses, already got new haircut, good makeup, new clothes and accessories.'''[42]

This sad shift from 1892 to 1982 is exactly the shift the Bible warns us from making. It is a shift from "good works" to "good looks." Consider God's instructions to His daughters: "I desire…likewise also that women should adorn themselves in respectable apparel, with modesty and self-control, not with braided hair and gold or pearls or costly attire, but with what is proper for women who profess godliness—with *good works*" (1 Tim. 2:8-10, emphasis added). God's accent for women is good works, not good looks.

What's your picture of the ideal woman? Go to any grocery store and on the cover of such magazines as *Self* or *Cosmopolitan* or *Glamour* (the titles alone are telling) you will find a glossy picture of the world's "ideal woman"—a scantily clad, skinny supermodel with a great career, neglected children, and another disintegrating marriage. These covers scream, "I'm the ideal woman! Be like me! Emulate me!" But Proverbs 31:10-31 describes the true model woman. In it, God says, "This is the ideal woman. Be like her. Emulate her."

First, consider this woman's noble character. "A wife of noble character who can find?" (Prov. 31:10a NIV). Implication: Not many. The very first thing mentioned about this woman is her noble character. This simple stress on character is quite countercultural. Our society is obsessed with image, while God is concerned with integrity. The world spends most of its time fixing the external. God's desire is that most of our time be spent fixing the internal. "Do not let your adorning be external—the braiding of hair, the wearing of gold, or the putting on of clothing—but let your adorning be the hidden person of the heart with the imperishable beauty of a gentle and quiet spirit, which in God's sight is very precious. For this is how the holy women who hoped in God used to adorn themselves, by submitting to their husbands" (1 Pet. 3:3-5). Women, the next time you get up in the morning and are having your devotional time, if your husband or children ask what you are doing, tell them, "I'm making myself beautiful." A woman of noble character is rare; she is also valuable. "She is worth far more than rubies" (Prov. 31:10b, NIV). Ladies, emulate this woman. Gentlemen, marry this kind of woman. This is a woman you can trust (vs. 11), and one who will bring you respect (vs. 23).

Second, look at the true ideal woman's work ethic. She does not lay on the sofa all day watching soap operas, while eating bonbons. This woman is the personification of hard work. "She rises while it is yet night and provides food for her household" (vs. 15). A little sweat doesn't frighten her, either. She works in the hot fields, which she purchased from her wise investments (vs. 16). Also, she makes a profit from her trading (vs. 18). "She looks well to the ways of her household and does not eat the bread of idleness. Her children rise up and call her blessed; her husband also, and he praises her" (vv. 27-28).

Finally, notice her fear of God. "Charm is deceptive, and beauty is vain, but a woman who fears the LORD is to be praised" (vs. 30). Her noble character and hard work are the outcome of her fear of God. She speaks with wisdom (vs. 26). Where does wisdom come from? "The fear of the LORD is the beginning of wisdom" (Prov. 9:10).

Proverbs was written "(t)o know wisdom and instruction" (Prov. 1:2). A description of the wife of noble character closes the book of Proverbs by providing us with an illustration of a person who has applied the teaching of Proverbs to her life with incredible results. "Give her of the fruit of her hands, and let her works praise her in the gates" (Prov. 31:31). Honoring a *woman* at the city gates wasn't usually done. But an unusual woman is worthy of unusual recognition.

29

WHOS'S REARING YOUR CHILDREN

Pondering the Priority of Parenting

Since the wisdom of Proverbs isn't automatically passed on to the next generation, I need to ask, "Who's rearing your children?" To make sure you understand the question correctly, let me tell you what I am *not* asking: I'm not asking, "Where do they sleep at night?" Or, "Who pays for their clothes, toys, and education?" I'm asking, "Who's rearing your children?" In other words, who is training and instructing them? Who is passing on to them beliefs, values, and convictions that they will adopt as their own when they become young adults and venture out on their own? I'm asking, "Whose influence is determining the trajectory of their entire earthly lives, and more importantly, their eternal destiny?" I hope you can see that when I ask, "Who's rearing your children?" I'm asking a monumental question.

The sad reality is that many children are rearing themselves. It's becoming increasingly common and acceptable to leave children—even young children—home alone. "Latchkey kids" is now part of our vocabulary. This tendency is tragic. The Bible says that all of us are born with a sin nature—a natural tendency toward evil. This is why children are naturally selfish and need to be taught to share their toys. They naturally lie and cover up their mistakes. Nobody has to teach a child how to lie. It comes from within. Children naturally get angry and whine when they don't get their way, and have to be taught repeatedly to be patient and self-controlled. If children are left to themselves, you can expect them to indulge their sinful desires with very little self-restraint.

The Minnesota Crime Commission reported back in the 1920s: "Every baby starts life as a little savage. He is completely selfish and self-centered. He wants what he wants when he wants it: his bottle, his mother's attention, his playmate's toys, his uncle's watch, or whatever. Deny him these and he seethes with rage and aggressiveness, which would be murderous were he not so helpless. He's dirty, he has no morals, no knowledge, no developed skills. This means that all children, not just certain children but all children, are born delinquent. If permitted to continue in their self-centered world of infancy, given free reign to their impulsive actions to satisfy each want, every child would grow up a criminal, a thief, a killer, a rapist." Again, let me ask, "Who's rearing your children?"

If you abdicate your responsibility, MTV and the Ozzy Osbourne family may take over. Isn't that a frightening thought! The average teenager watches three hours of television a day. Meanwhile, our young people reported that they spend less than four minutes a day in meaningful conversation with their mothers, and a mere two and a half minutes a day talking things over with Dad. Get this: Teens spend 2,800% more time watching TV than they do with Mom and Dad. And we haven't even considered the impact of music, video games, or the Internet. Who did you say is rearing your children?

In Deuteronomy 5, we have the declaration of the Ten Commandments. Then Moses tells the Israelites: '"And these words that I command you today shall be on your heart. You shall teach them diligently to your children, and shall talk of them when you sit in your house, and when you walk by the way, and when you lie down, and when you rise"' (Deut. 6:6-7). At least two parenting principles emerge from these verses.

First, apply the word of God in your own life. The commandments "shall be on your heart." I take this to mean that parents should learn the Bible, love the Bible, and live according to the Bible. If you haven't learned the commands, how can you teach your children? If you don't love the Bible, do you really think your children will see how precious it is? If you don't live according to God's Word, can you expect your children to submit to its authority? Parenting begins by being a godly example, because of who we *are*. This principle is crucial, since values are better caught than taught. I'm a Chicago White Sox fan. Guess what team my kids cheer for? Our children will naturally adopt many of our values by simple imitation.

Second, impress the Word of God upon your children. Make it an intentional priority to ground your children in the truth. Parents have the primary responsibility to instruct their children in the faith. And parents, not pastors or teachers, will stand before God and give the ultimate account for how they reared their children. To teach your children diligently just read and talk about the Word constantly—"when you sit in your house, and when you walk by the way, and when you lie down, and when you rise." This takes *time* and presupposes you are doing things together as a tight-knit family. And please don't be deluded by the "quality time" myth. You might think the two and a half minutes are quality, but I guarantee you your kids will feel short-changed. Too many parents are consumed with their careers, and they're unwittingly sacrificing the souls of their children on the altar of materialism. Go home early and spend some quantity time with your children.

30

A FATHER'S LEGACY

Considering the Influence Fathers Can Have for Generations

While the role of a mother is indispensable (Pro. 31:1), Proverbs focuses on the father's responsibility to instruct his children (4:1). You may have noticed that in the last few decades a disturbing trend has been taking place on television sitcoms. Twenty or 30 years ago, Dad was the most dignified and respected member of the family. Ward Cleaver (played by the late pastor Hugh Beaumont) on *"Leave It to Beaver"* was loved, admired, and respected by his wife and two sons. Also, consider the fathers of "*Little House on the Prairie*," "*Father Knows Best,*" and "*The Waltons.*" Today, Dad is the biggest idiot in the family. See "*The Simpsons*" and "*Married...with Children*" for starters. I believe this is Satan's attempt to undermine the crucial role that fathers play in God's design for the family.

Here is a solemn truth to reckon with: *The coming generations will reap what their fathers have sown.* After God gave the Israelites the second commandment, forbidding idolatry (Deut. 5:8-9a), He went on to give them a negative and a positive consequence to underscore the serious nature of the command: '"(F)or I the LORD your God am a jealous God, visiting the iniquity of the fathers on the children to *the third and fourth generation* of those who hate me" ' " (5:9b, emphasis added). God tells fathers that their children, grandchildren, great-grandchildren, and great-great-grandchildren may be affected by the fathers' sin. How? Many ways are possible, but one way is by passing along each father's sinful way to the following generations. Do any of you struggle with the same sin(s) as your father? I know my children do.

Before you fall into the mire of misery, let me mention the positive consequence that also follows the second commandment: " ' "but showing steadfast love to *thousands* of those who love me and keep my commandments" ' " (Deut. 5:10, emphasis added). What an awesome contrast: three or four generations as opposed to a thousand generations (see also Deut. 7:9). If this isn't influence, then I don't know what is. Think of it. If you love God and keep His commandments, a thousand generations may reap what you have sown. Talk about a lasting legacy!

This generational Jewish mindset is very different from our typical individualistic American mindset. We Americans tend to think—wrongly—that what we do doesn't affect anybody except ourselves. When Solomon became king over Israel, he realized that it was a direct result of his father David's faithfulness (1 Kgs. 3:6). Even after the death of Solomon, God continued to deal with succeeding kings based on His relationship with David (1 Kgs. 11:12-13; 34-36).

Several false applications could be derived from this teaching. First, because Deuteronomy 5:9 addresses "fathers" and not "mothers," let us not conclude that women or mothers have no lasting influence. It seems that Paul's disciple Timothy became a Christian through the influence of his grandmother Lois and mother Eunice (2 Tim. 1:5). Personally, I can testify that I'm a Christian—from a human perspective—due to the direct impact of my godly mother. Second, this teaching should not result in a defeatist or fatalistic attitude, which says, "I'm destined to be like this because my father (or grandfather) was like this." Jesus Christ came to earth so that we could be set free from our father's sin and become new creations (2 Cor. 5:17). By the grace of God we can renounce the sins of our fathers, and begin a new godly line. Third, if you or your children do not have a father, do not assume that you or they are doomed. There is great hope, for God promises that He Himself will be "Father of the fatherless" (Ps. 68:5). You couldn't ask for a better father.

Several years ago *Christian Life and Faith* magazine presented some interesting results as it contrasted the generations coming from two different families. The Jukes family legacy began in 1677 when an immoral man married a very licentious woman. Nineteen hundred descendants came from that union. Of these, 771 were criminals, 250 were arrested for various offenses, 60 were thieves, and 39 were convicted for murder. Forty of the women were known to have a venereal disease. These people spent a combined total of 1,300 years behind bars, and cost the State of New York nearly 3 million dollars.

The second family was the Edwards family. The third generation included Jonathan Edwards who was the great New England pastor and theologian. Of the 1,344 descendants, many were college presidents and professors. One hundred eighty-six became ministers of the Gospel, and many others were active in their churches. Eighty-six were state senators, three were Congressmen, 30 were judges, and one became Vice President of the United States. No reference was made of anyone spending time in jail.

God still says, " ' "Oh that they had such a mind as this always, to fear me and to keep all my commandments, that it might go well with them and with their descendants forever!" ' " (Deut. 5:29).

NOTES

[1] John Piper, *The Pleasures of God* (Portland, Oregon: Multnomah, 1991), 211.

[2] Quoted in Warren W. Wiersbe, *Preaching and Teaching with Imagination* (Grand Rapids, MI: Baker Books, 2002), 64.

[3] David Mills, "Enchanting Children" in *Touchstone,* Dec. 2006, 20-21.

[4] *Ibid., 21.*

[5] Jonathan Edwards, *The Freedom of the Will* (Portland, PA: Soli Deo Gloria Publications, 1996), 4, 6.

[6] Steve Wilkins, *Call of Duty*, (Nashville, Tennessee: Cumberland House Publishing, Inc., 1997), 64.

[7] John Murray, *Principles of Conduct* (Grand Rapids, Michigan: William B. Eerdmans Publishing Co., 2001), 231.

[8] *Ibid.*

[9] John Calvin, *Institutes of the Christian Religion,* (Philadelphia, PA: The Westminster Press, MCMLX) Book 1, 42-43.

[10] Jonathan Edwards, *The Religious Affections* (Carlisle, Pennsylvania: The Banner of Truth Trust, 1994), 108.

[11] I'm greatly indebted to Norm Wakefield for pointing out the following implications and showing how our culture has

encouraged and fostered this type of independent, rebellious thinking.

[12] Steve Wilkins, *Face to Face* (Moscow, ID: Canon Press, 2002), 22.

[13] Murray Harris, *The Expositor's Bible Commentary* (Grand Rapids, MI: Zondervan Publishing House, 1995), 187, emphasis added..

[14] Wisdom is personified as a woman and not a man, since the Hebrew word for wisdom, *sophia*, is feminine.

[15] Nancy Wilson, *Building Her House* (Moscow, ID: Canon Press, 2006) 85.

[16] *Ibid.*, 86.

[17] John Piper, *Taste and See* (Portland, Oregon: Multnomah, 2005) 356-357.

[18] Douglas Moo, *James* (Grand Rapids, Michigan: William B. Eerdmans Publishing Co., 1993), 78.

[19] From the *Autobiography of George Muller*, quoted in *Taste and See*, by John Piper, 267-268.

[20] J.I. Packer, *Evangelism & the Sovereignty of God* (Downers Grove, Illinois; Inter-Varsity Press, 1961), 18-19.

[21] Douglas Wilson, *Future Men* (Moscow, ID: Canon Press, 2001) 63.

[22] Quoted on bible.org Web site, from an Oct. 17, 1977, *People* magazine article

[23] James Patterson and Peter Kim, *The Day America Told the Truth (Upper Saddle River, NJ: Prentice Hall Trade, 1919)* 65-66 (As a funny side note, the title is ironic since the survey also revealed that most Americans don't tell the truth).

[24] Will and Ariel Durant, *The Lessons of History*, (New York, NY: MJF Books, 1997) 81.

[25] Charles Bridges, *Proverbs* (Carlisle, Pennsylvania: The Banner of Truth Trust, 1998), 487.

[26] Janet L. Folger, *The Criminalization of Christianity* (Sisters, Oregon: Multnomah Publishers, Inc., 2005), 14-15.
[27] See "MTV" by John MacArthur Jr., on Google.
[28] C.S. Lewis, *Mere Christianity*, (San Francisco, CA: HarperOne, 2001) 121-122.
[29] *Ibid.*, p. 122
[30] Gilbert K. Chesterton, *Heretics/Orthodoxy* (Nashville, TN: Thomas Nelson, Inc., 2000)
[31] C.S. Lewis, *Mere Christianity* (San Francisco, CA: HarperOne, 2001) 124-125.
[32] The five examples cited are all from Janet Folger, *The Criminalization of Christianity* (Sisters, Oregon: Multnomah Publishers, Inc., 2005), 101-103
[33] Gary DeMar, *America's Christian History* (Powder Springs, Georgia: American Vision, 1995) p. 27.
[34] Alexander Strauch, *Leading With Love* (Littleton, Colorado: Lewis and Roth Publishers, 2006), 175-176.
[35] Janet Folger, *The Criminalization of Christianity* (Sisters, Oregon: Multnomah Publishers, Inc., 2005), 103.
[36] Charles Spurgeon, *Lectures To My Students* (Grand Rapids, MI: Zondervan Publishing House, 1954) 162-163.
[37] Larry Crabb, *Inside Out* (Colorado Springs, Colorado: NavPress, 1988) 133.
[38] *Ibid.*, 135-136.
[39] Martyn Lloyd-Jones, *Spiritual Depression* (Grand Rapids, Michigan: William B. Eerdmans Publishing Co., 1964), 20-21.
[40] R.C. Sproul, *The Holiness of God* (Wheaton, Illinois: Tyndale House Publishers, 1998) 66-67.
[41] *Ibid.*, 67-68.
[42] John Piper, *A Godward Life* (Portland, Oregon: Multnomah, 2001) 62.

Scripture Index

Leviticus

Numbers

Deuteronomy

Judges

1 Samuel

2 Samuel

1 Kings

2 Chronicles

Job

Psalms

Proverbs

Ecclesiastes

Isaiah

Jeremiah

Daniel

Amos

Nahum

Matthew

Mark

Luke

John

Acts

Romans

1 Corinthians

2 Corinthians

Galatians

Ephesians

Philippians

Colossians

1 Thessalonians

2 Thessalonians

1 Timothy

2 Timothy

Titus

Hebrews

1 Peter

1 John

Revelation

Biblical

teaching

must be vivid,

inform the mind,

provoke the imagination

and stir the emotions

and move the will

Thoreau—

A Fact

Baldly

Stated

is dry

It must

Be the

vehicle

of

some

humanity.

Deep places

are not

reached by

instruction

But rather

stories, illustrations

and proverbs

LaVergne, TN USA
30 July 2010

191574LV00001B/14/P

9 781609 572945